Children's Daily Prayer For Summer

By Elizabeth McMahon Jeep

**Daily Prayer for the Home and Other Settings
including Prayers for Each Day of June, July and August
with Meal Prayers, Morning and Night Prayers
and Special Prayers for Birthdays and Other Occasions**

LTP

LITURGY
TRAINING
PUBLICATIONS

ACKNOWLEDGMENTS

Readings from the Old Testament and New Testament, except as noted below, are taken from the *Contemporary English Version* of the Bible, copyright © 1991 American Bible Society, 1875 Broadway, New York NY 10023, and are used by permission of the American Bible Society. All rights reserved.

Readings from the book of Wisdom are taken from the *New Revised Standard Version* of the Bible, copyright © 1989, Division of Christian Education of the National Council of the Churches of Christ in the United States of America. Used with permission. All rights reserved.

Psalm texts are adapted from the *New Revised Standard Version* of the Bible, copyright © 1989, Division of Christian Education of the National Council of the Churches of Christ in the United States of America. Used with permission. All rights reserved. These texts originally appeared in P*salms for Praise and Worship,* © 1992, Abingdon Press.

Excerpts from the English translation of the *Angelus* from *A Book of Prayers,* copyright © 1982 International Committee on English in the Liturgy, Inc.(ICEL); excerpts from the English translation of the *Book of Blessings,* copyright © 1988 United States Catholic Conference, Washington, D.C.. Used with permission. All rights reserved.

English translation of the Glory to the Father by the International Consultation on English Texts (ICET).

Texts taken from *Catholic Household Blessings and Prayers,* copyright © 1988 United States Catholic Conference, Washington, D.C., are used with permission. All rights reserved.

CHILDREN'S DAILY PRAYER FOR SUMMER, copyright 2000 Archdiocese of Chicago: Liturgy Training Publications, 1800 North Hermitage Avenue, Chicago IL 60622-1101. All rights reserved.

Order phone: 1-800-933-1800
Editorial phone: 1-773-486-8970
Fax: 1-800-933-7094

CHILDREN'S DAILY PRAYER FOR SUMMER was illustrated by Carolina Arentsen. The book was edited by Kathy Luty and Gabe Huck. Audrey Novak Riley was the production editor. The design is by Mary Bowers and M. Urgo. The book was typeset by Jim Mellody-Pizzato in Gill Sans and Sabon and printed by Webcom Limited in Toronto, Ontario.

ISBN 1-56854-356-5

CDPSUM
$8.00

CONTENTS

INTRODUCTION

Christians recognize the sacredness of the hours of the day and the seasons of the year. This book is for families who honor that tradition and intend to pray together in the wonderful days of summer. Summer is a marvel to us who live in the northern hemisphere. The warmth of sunshine is reflected on our faces, the lightness of our clothing is mirrored in the lightness of our spirit, the break in routine is greeted with an openness to the neighbor and to the world. Even Americans, considered to be the most goal-oriented people on the planet, savor summer's idleness and make room for the spontaneous and unexpected. In that joyful spirit we fashion words and rituals of praise and thanksgiving.

This book is also intended for classrooms and other places where groups of people come together during the summer. It is much like the annual volumes of *Children's Daily Prayer* that are used in many schools. If you are using this book in these larger settings, you may wish to read the introduction and notes in that book.

Parts of This Book

This book includes many resources for prayer, many more than one family will use in a single summer. Take some time now to look at the table of contents and to page through parts of the book.

Simple prayers for morning and bedtime are conveniently placed on the inside front cover. Meal prayers for weekdays and Sundays are on the inside back cover. These are printed where they are easy to find each day, and you may also want to tape a copy of the morning and bedtime prayers to the bathroom mirror or refrigerator door.

Each of the three summer months is given a short introduction to help prepare for the days to come. In addition, there is a psalm designated for the whole month, so that those who use this book may begin to learn it by heart. After the psalm come the pages for all the days of the month.

Each day follows the same order of prayer: an introduction (having to do with a saint or the season), the psalm (which can be prayed back-and-forth, with one person reading the leader's part and the others reading the part designated "all"), a scripture reading, questions for reflection, a closing prayer and finally the Lord's Prayer.

There are many days and events during the summer that call for special prayers or blessings. This book offers pages for the church's three summer solemnities: The Birth of John the Baptist on June 24 (page 39), Saints Peter and Paul on June 29 (page 44), and the Assumption of the Virgin Mary on August 15 (page 98)—a holy day in the United States. A Blessing for Father's Day is on page 4. Other occasions for which prayers or blessings are included are: birthdays (page 2), times of sadness or trouble (page 3), days when reconciliation and peacemaking are needed (page 5), travel days (page 8), family gatherings (page 9), or days when there is enough rain, or too much or too little (page 6).

Preparing for Sunday

On Sundays, the family goes to church to participate in the liturgical assembly. Every Sunday, we hear the word of God proclaimed, reading through the scriptures bit by bit, Sunday after Sunday. In this book, one scripture reading from each Sunday of the summer is included among the daily scripture readings. The family can look for that reading before Sunday comes and reflect upon it in advance. This will help them be better prepared to take an active role in the celebration. Families who prepare themselves in advance find it easier to be attentive at church. As time goes on, they build a valuable habit of reflecting on what is proclaimed and celebrated.

An index of the readings for each Sunday likely to fall during the summer is on page 117. Determine the liturgical title of the Sunday (the parish's bulletin will usually include that information), look for it in the index, and then turn to that page and read the scripture passage. Point out to the children that the passages from scripture in this book are actual translations of the original texts, just like the translation proclaimed in church. This one just uses simpler language.

The Minimum Daily Requirement

Most of us lay persons need two related things to nourish our spiritual selves, just as we need vitamins and minerals to nourish our physical selves. First, we need four "moments" of organized, "formal" prayer each day. Second, we need a prayerful attitude that moves with us through the day just beneath the surface, an attitude that rises to consciousness when we are alone. These two forms of prayer nourish and support each other. They help us to form a family that is a prayerful community, not just a household where a number of Christians happen to exist together.

This is not to say that participation in the Sunday assembly is not equally essential to the Christian spirit. Keeping Sunday holy is a nonnegotiable element of our lives, whether at home or on our travels. But we must come to that assembly as prayerful people, ready to celebrate with the parish community. The Sunday celebration is not magic. Alone, it is unable to complete the task of forming us as Christians.

The four minimum "moments" of prayer are these:

1. A dedication of the day on rising (see Prayer for Morning on the inside front cover); this might be said individually or together, aloud, at the breakfast table.
2. Prayer before meals (see the Meal Prayers for Weekdays and Sundays on the inside back cover).
3. An uninterrupted time of prayer together as a whole family (see the dated pages for June, July and August; "Preparing for Sunday" on page 116; and the prayers for Occasions on pages 2 to 11); this should be given at least 10 or 15 minutes.

4. A prayer before sleep (see Prayer before Bedtime on the inside front cover); this traditionally includes thanksgiving for the events of the day and an examination of conscience.

A Family Commitment

"Uninterrupted time of prayer together as a whole family" (number 3 above) requires some frank conversation and negotiation before being adopted or abandoned. If some members leave for work while others are still asleep, it may be better to choose a time after dinner for this prayer, that includes reading and reflecting on a passage of scripture. Some families choose to extend the meal prayer (while keeping the meal hot!). Other families dedicate one evening a week to their life together, turning off the TV, ignoring the phone, and then playing family games and good music after an unhurried time of prayer.

It is wise to discuss your summer plans at a family meeting before introducing this book. How and how often do you pray together now? How can traditions already established be strengthened? Are there things that regularly interfere with your chosen times of prayer? If you could control the world, how and when would you pray? How can lives and schedules be simplified? What sacrifices will family prayer require? It is said that it takes people 21 days to substitute a new habit for an old one; are you willing to work at a new plan for at least 21 days before deciding whether or not to keep on with it? Is family prayer looked upon as one person's idea and therefore that person's sole responsibility to prepare, to remind, to lead? Any resistance should be faced and discussed honestly and gently. It may not be possible to clear up all the issues at one meeting. Patience and cooperation are needed from everyone if prayer is not to become a source of frustration or controversy.

Disciplined but Flexible

The structure of daily prayer suggested in this book is founded on readings and psalms from the Bible. Work with this structure until it becomes clear that something else might be more comfortable for the family. Use the special blessings and prayers when the summer days call for them.

But flexibility is the soul of family life! Use whichever parts of the daily pages seem comfortable. You may substitute songs and hymns for some of the prayers or psalms. If you like a story, you can repeat it rather than moving on to the next page.

From a young age, children should take an active role in the prayer, and not remain hearers only. They relish lighting candles, sprinkling holy water, blessing seeds or food or pets. They can learn to prepare the reading and proclaim the scripture with dignity. Children are

natural liturgists, and quickly learn when to wait for silences and when to resume.

On the other hand, regularity is also the soul of family life! Plan ahead. How can you be consistent without being rigid? What systems will help you keep your promises? Where will you keep this book so that it is available but not underfoot? What activities might call for adjusting the time of prayer? What will you do if the phone rings or a friend drops in? How will you pray on trips? How will you rotate leadership, giving everyone a role in the prayer?

Several things can help:

1. Have a regular place for prayer. It may be the dining room table, or it can be a special place with a cross and images of saints, flowers, holy water from church, candles.

2. Have a regular posture for prayer. If possible, sit down for the reading and reflection and discussion. Stand up for the prayers at the end. Lift your hands high during the Lord's Prayer. Make the sign of the cross at the beginning and the end. Night prayer is often prayed kneeling by one's bed.

3. Always sing something. It may be a favorite hymn or chant or refrain sung at the beginning of prayer or after the reading, or it may be a simple alleluia (learned from Sunday Mass) at the end. The Lord's Prayer itself may be sung, as it often is at Mass.

Community prayer is never as easy as praying alone: Members of religious communities can tell you that. But common prayer will strengthen bonds among family members, and deepen mutual respect and understanding. The Lord himself has reminded us, "Whenever two or three of you come together in my name, I am there with you." (Matthew 18:20)

Themes of Summer Prayer

It is hoped that the daily introductions will reinforce our understanding of the communion of saints. We are members of a religious family with a long tradition; our people have been through good times and bad. They have left the scriptures and the witness of their lives to us so that we may find it a little easier to follow in Jesus' footsteps. Some of these saints will become your particular friends, others will not. That is all right. The point is to listen to the story that each one has to tell.

You will hear about some new people this summer. The days that are not dedicated to major saints have been used to introduce men and women whose stories are not as well known. Many of them are women. In past ages, women's lives were often restricted to the home or the convent. Few of them had the kinds of adventures that attract attention and get one's name in the "public" list of saints. But they have great wisdom to share.

Many prayers in this book focus on thanksgiving for the earth and its creatures, and the key signs of summer: sun, water, earth. It is good to remember the fragility of our environment and encourage respect for the earth. We are also reminded to care for others, and look upon all people with respect. That is a theme for any time of year.

OCCASIONS

A Blessing for Birthdays

 all make
the sign
of the cross

LEADER   Loving God,
     you created all the people of the world,
     and you know each of us by name.
   We thank you for N.,
     who celebrates *his/her* birthday.
   Bless *him/her* with your love and friendship
     that *he/she* may grow in wisdom,
     knowledge, and grace.
   May *he/she* love *his/her* family always
     and be ever faithful to *his/her* friends.
   We ask this through Christ our Lord.

ALL   **Amen.**

 those present may place
a hand on the head or shoulders
of the person being blessed

LEADER   May God, in whose presence our ancestors walked,
     bless you.

ALL   **Amen.**

LEADER   May God, who has been your shepherd from birth until now,
     keep you.

ALL   **Amen.**

LEADER   May God, who saves you from all harm,
     give you peace.

ALL   **Amen.**

 all make
the sign
of the cross

adapted from *Catholic Household Blessings and Prayers*

Prayers for Sad Days

These are prayers for sad days and other times of trouble. Each one can be memorized and used when it is needed. To pray as a group, you can begin with the sign of the cross, then read one of the passages from scripture, and end with the prayer and sign of the cross.

Psalm 18:29

You, O Lord, are my lamp;
my God, you make my darkness bright.

Psalm 27:13–14

I believe that I shall see the goodness
    of the Lord
in the land of the living!
Wait for the Lord;
be strong, and let your heart take courage.
Wait for the Lord.

Psalm 28:7

The Lord is my strength and shield
in whom my heart trusts;
so I am helped, and my heart rejoices,
and with my song I give thanks to the Lord.

Psalm 91:14–16

Those who cling to me in love I will deliver;
I will protect them, because they know
    my name.
When they call me, I will answer them;
I will be with them in trouble,
I will rescue them and honor them.
I will satisfy them with long life
and show them my salvation.

Isaiah 41:10

Do not fear, for I am with you.
Do not be afraid, for I am your God;
I will strengthen you, I will help you,
I will hold you in my hand.

Prayer

Most holy and most merciful God,
    strength of the weak,
    rest for the weary,
    comfort of the sorrowful,
    our refuge in every time of need:
Grant us strength and protect us.
Support us in all dangers,
    and carry us through all trials.

We ask this through Christ our Lord. **Amen.**

 all make
the sign
of the cross

A Blessing for Father's Day

The giving of a fatherly blessing is an ancient custom. Among the Jews, the blessing served as a "last will and testament" and great importance was put on it. Christian blessings usually ask God to bless someone with some spiritual benefit. The particular grace asked for is usually suited to the life, personality or needs of the one being blessed.

Preparation: Fathers, grandfathers, stepfathers and godfathers being honored should look at examples of blessings in scripture, so that they can compose an appropriate blessing for each of their children. See, for example, Genesis 1:26–31 (God blesses Adam and Eve), Genesis 27 (Isaac blesses Jacob and Esau), Genesis 49 (Israel blesses his sons), John 14:27–28 and John 17: 24–26 (Jesus blesses his apostles), Ephesians 6:23–24, 1 Thessalonians 5:23–24, and 2 Thessalonians 3:16 (Paul blesses the Christian community).

Children (of both generations) should prepare prayers of gratitude for their fathers. Young children might use the formula included below to help them organize their thoughts. They might say, for example, "Blessed are you, Lord God, for my father who loves me" or "... for a father who is happy and funny." These prayers can be written on Father's Day cards.

The ritual can be done at the dinner table or before presenting Father's Day cards or gifts.

▶ all make
the sign
of the cross

LEADER
Blessed be God,
from whom all fatherhood,
both in heaven and on earth,
takes its name. **Amen.**

CHILD
Blessed are you, Lord our God,
for giving me a father who. . . .

▶ additional children take their turns
blessing God for their father

FATHER

▶ the father goes to each child,
puts his hands on that child's head,
and offers the blessing he has prepared

▶ repeat the ceremony
with grandfathers and other fatherly person

LEADER
In our love
may we try always
to strengthen one another
and give glory to God.

Let us pray with the words that Jesus taught u

Our Father . . .

▶ sing
"alleluia"

4

Prayers of Reconciliation and Peace

Prayer after an Argument

READING

Isaiah 2:15–16, 17

Listen to the words of the prophet Isaiah.
The LORD says this:
No matter how much you pray, I won't listen.
You are too violent.
Wash yourselves clean!
Stop doing wrong and learn to live right.
See that justice is done.
I, the LORD, invite you to come and talk it over.

The word of the Lord.

DIALOGUE

 after a few minutes of silence;
begin with these
or similar words

We may now speak of the wrong we have done
and the good we have not done,
that regret may come from the heart,
and forgiveness be freely given.

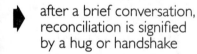 after a brief conversation,
reconciliation is signified
by a hug or handshake

CLOSING

Gracious Lord,
you are slow to anger, full of love,
good in every way, merciful to every creature.
Forgive our sins and strengthen our weakness,
that we may praise you
through Christ our Lord. **Amen.**

Let us pray with the words that Jesus taught us:
Our Father . . .

 sing
"alleluia"

The Confiteor

I confess to almighty God,
and to you, my brothers and sisters,
that I have sinned through my own fault
in my thoughts and in my words,
in what I have done,
and in what I have failed to do;
and I ask blessed Mary, ever virgin,
all the angels and saints,
and you, my brothers and sisters,
to pray for me to the Lord our God.

Prayer for Peace

Lord, make me an instrument of your peace:
where there is hatred, let me sow love;
where there is injury, pardon;
where there is doubt, faith;
where there is despair, hope;
where there is darkness, light;
where there is sadness, joy.
O divine Master,
grant that I may not so much seek
to be consoled as to console,
to be understood as to understand,
to be loved as to love.
For it is in giving that we receive,
it is in pardoning that we are pardoned,
it is in dying that we are born to eternal life.

Psalm 133:1

Behold, how good and pleasant it is
when kindred live together in unity!

Prayers about Rain

Thanksgiving for Rain

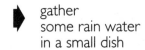
gather
some rain water
in a small dish

We give you thanks, God our Creator,
    for the gift of this water.
Rain to clean the air.
Rain to cool the sidewalks.
Rain to nourish the flowers and trees.
Rain to fill the rivers and streams.
Rain to make leaves sparkle
    and cobwebs dance.
Rain on windows and umbrellas,
Rain for a thirsty world.

> parts can be added
> to the litany of thanksgiving

Loving God, you make us joyful
    with your gift of rain.

> all dip a hand in the water
> and make
> the sign of the cross

Prayer for Rain when the Ground is Dry

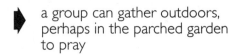
a group can gather outdoors,
perhaps in the parched garden
to pray

Loving God, the world is thirsty
    for your saving rain.
Crops wither, animals weaken.
Your children fear for the harvest.
As once you saved us
    through the waters of baptism
so now remember your loving kindness,
    and send us rain.
We ask this through Christ our Lord. **Amen.**

> sprinkle water on the garden and grass
> and each other
> with chants and dancing

Prayer in Time of Flooding

Lord God, through the power of your Spirit,
    you brought life from water
        at the time of creation,
    saved Noah's family from the flood,
    led the Israelites dry-footed through the sea,
    and raised us, reborn,
        from the waters of baptism.
So now, send your Spirit
    to rescue *us/the people of* _____
        from the threatening flood.
Protect *us/them,* and give *us/them* peace.
We ask this through Christ our Lord. **Amen.**

6

Prayers for the Garden and Its Gifts

Prayer for a Newly Planted Garden

➤ pray the Psalm for June (on page 15)
in the midst of the garden

READING
Genesis 1:11 – 13

Listen to the words of the book of Genesis.
God said, "I command the earth to produce all kinds of plants, including fruit trees and grain." And that's what happened. The earth produced all kinds of vegetation. God looked at what he had done, and it was good. Evening came and then morning—that was the third day.

The word of the Lord.

➤ sing many "alleluias"
as you water
the newly planted seeds

Prayer for Growing Things

➤ pray about what you see
as you water or weed the garden
in words like these:

For all the gifts of the earth:
Glory to you, O Lord.
For seeds and bulbs that we planted:
Glory to you, O Lord.
For sunshine that makes the leaves green:
Glory to you, O Lord.
For tomato plants already sprouting:
Glory to you, O Lord.
(and so on)

➤ when your job is done
end your prayer

Glory to the Father, and to the Son,
and to the Holy Spirit:
as it was in the beginning, is now,
and will be for ever. Amen. Alleluia.

Harvest Blessing

Gather some fruits or vegetables from your garden, or from a farmers' market. Prepare some for eating and place the rest in a bowl on the table, along with a bowl of holy water.

Praise is due to you, O God.
Psalm 65:1a, 9–11

You visit the earth and water it,
you greatly enrich it;
you provide the people with grain,
for so you have prepared it.

You water its furrows abundantly,
settling its ridges,
softening it with showers,
and blessing its growth.

You crown the year with your bounty.

 sprinkle the fruits and vegetables
and the people holding them
with holy water

Bless us, O Lord, in these fruits and vegetables
of the summer season.
May all who taste them be filled with joy;
and may they be for us
a sign of that final harvest
when all creation is gathered
into your kingdom. **Amen.**

 all make the sign of the cross
and then enjoy the food!

A Blessing for Travelers

Blessing before a Journey

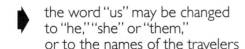 the word "us" may be changed
to "he," "she" or "them,"
or to the names of the travelers

Loving God, source of all life and joy,
    be with *us* as we travel,
    make *us* respectful of those *we* meet,
    grateful for those who offer hospitality,
    patient and kind to one another,
    alert to the wonders of your world,
    and confident in new situations.
Remind *us* daily of your loving presence,
    and bring *us* safely home. **Amen.**

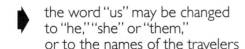 stretch your hands out
toward those who are preparing to leave;
if all are leaving, hold hands

May the Lord bless *us* and keep *us*,
May the Lord's face shine upon *us*
and guide *our* feet into the way of peace. **Amen.**

Thanksgiving after a Journey

Blessed are you, Lord our God,
    Creator of the earth and its wonders.
We thank you for a safe journey [for _____
    and a place to call home.
Lead us along your paths in this life,
    and gather us into your heavenly dwelling.
We ask this through Christ our Lord. **Amen.**

Let us pray with the words that Jesus taught u

Our Father . . .

 sing
"alleluia"

Don't forget to take this book along on your trip! Y
will want to pray each day of the journey.

Prayers for Gatherings of Families and Friends

During the summer we often visit relatives or friends. We may even go to a family reunion and see aunts, uncles and cousins we do not see during the school year. This might be a large group spending a weekend at the beach, or just a few people gathered at Grandmother's bedside. There is usually picture-taking and story-telling, and the sharing of good food. At such times it is good to remember that we are gathered by God's grace. A simple ritual and a short prayer are best.

Reunion Blessing

A toast is a traditional way to interrupt the conversations, welcome everyone, focus on the meaning of the gathering and provide an official beginning. Wine is the usual drink for a toast, but juice, milk or water will do.

 see that everyone
has something to drink
and is ready for the toast

LEADER

welcome everyone;
introduce newcomers;
mention those who are missing;
tell a joke or two, perhaps;
then ask everyone to hold out their glasses
and pray:

In the joy of our gathering,
in the strength of our friendship
in the sharing of life
may God be praised:
Blessed be God for ever.

ALL
Blessed be God for ever.

A Ceremonial Conversation

Each person lights a candle and tells something that has made them thankful, joyful or hopeful since the last reunion. After everyone has taken a turn, a candle is lighted for those who are not present, and they are named.

Instead of candles, you may want to use stones, shells or wildflowers gathered nearby.

LEADER
Let us reflect for a moment
on the blessings we have experienced
and the stories we have shared.

 allow a moment
of silence

Let us bless the Lord
who is with us and in us:
source of our joy,
center of our hope,
companion in our sorrow.
Blessed be God for ever.

ALL
Blessed be God for ever.

conclude
with the Lord's Prayer
or a familiar hymn

Family Theme Song

Choose a hymn that the whole family likes and be sure that everyone knows it. It can become a family theme song, used whenever there is a birth, graduation, marriage or death to be commemorated. A ceremonial copy can be handed on to each new in-law, along with other family traditions.

9

Prayers for the Sick

Theotokos

Holy Mary, Mother of God,
  pray for all who are sick,
  especially _____.

Mother of Mercy,	**pray for them.**
Mother of Light,	**pray for them.**
Mother of the Savior,	**pray for them.**
Mother of the Good Shepherd,	**pray for them.**
Mother of the Church,	**pray for them.**

Lord God, through the prayers of Mary,
  our Mother,
bring your healing presence
    to all who are sick, injured or troubled.
We ask this through Christ our Lord. **Amen.**

You see our troubles, Lord;
  you know our suffering.
In your mercy strengthen all the sick.
Ease their pain,
  heal their bodies,
  brighten their loneliness and
  calm their fears.
Let them know you are always near,
  their healer and redeemer.

**In the name of the Father,
  and of the Son,
  and of the Holy Spirit. Amen.**

Isaiah 40:29 – 31

The LORD gives strength to those who
    are weary,
even young people get tired,
    then stumble and fall.
But those who trust the LORD
    will find new strength.
They will be strong like eagles
    soaring upward on wings;
they will walk and run without getting tired.

Psalm 10:12, 14

Arise, O LORD; O God, lift up your hand;
do not forget the afflicted.
You note trouble and grief,
that you may take it into your hands;
the helpless commit themselves to you.

Prayer of Saint Augustine *(adapted)*

Watch, O Lord, with those who wake,
    or watch or weep tonight.
Tend your sick ones.
Rest your weary ones.
Bless your dying ones.
Soothe your suffering ones.
Pity your afflicted ones,
for your love's sake, O Lord Christ. **Amen.**

A Blessing of Pets

We usually spend more time with our pets during the summer than we do during the school year. You may want to show appreciation for the friendship and enjoyment they give you by asking God's protection for them.

An image of Saint Francis can be put in a place of honor. For this blessing, one leader and two readers are needed. Begin and end with a song, such as "All creatures of our God and king."

 all make
the sign
of the cross

LEADER
Let us bless the Lord,
now and for ever.

ALL
Amen.

LEADER
Animals fill the skies, the earth and the seas. They are God's beloved creatures. Saint Francis remembered this. He called the animals his brothers and sisters.

Today we ask God to bless these animals, our brothers and sisters. We thank God for letting us share the earth with such wonderful and amazing creatures.

FIRST READER   Genesis 1:20–21
Listen to the words of the book of Genesis.

God said, "I command the ocean to be full of living creatures, and I command birds to fly above the earth." So God made the giant sea monsters and all the living creatures that swim in the ocean. He also made every kind of bird. God looked at what he had done, and it was good.

SECOND READER   Genesis 1:24–25
God said, "I command the earth to give life to all kinds of tame animals, wild animals, and reptiles." And that's what happened. God made every one of them. Then he looked at what he had done, and it was good.

The word of the Lord.

LEADER
O God our creator,
everything that has the breath of life
gives you praise!

 hold out one hand
over the animals
in blessing, and say:

Lord, with love and compassion,
watch over our pets and all animals.
Keep them in good health.
Guard them against trouble.

May the wisdom of Saint Francis
and our love for these animals
deepen our respect for all your creation.
We ask this through Christ our Lord.

ALL
Amen.

 all make
the sign
of the cross

JUNE

THE MONTH OF JUNE

The sixth month on our calendar is a month of changes. The weather becomes reliably sunny and pleasant in the northern hemisphere, and it almost demands that we spend more time out of doors. So we welcome the end of the school year and the beginning of vacation time. We begin many things in June, such as summer gardens, team sports, and summer chores. Because we spend more time at home, it is natural to help with more of the work.

The month is named for Juno. In Roman myths, Juno was the goddess of hearth and home. The hearth is the fireplace, which was once the gathering spot for cooking, conversation and storytelling. During June we often gather around the barbecue and enjoy family picnics. Because of June's connection with home and family life, it is a traditional month for weddings.

In the northern hemisphere, June is the month of the summer solstice, when we experience the longest period of sunlight. This time is called *midsummer,* even though we are just beginning many of our summer activities. This reminds us that time is a gift that we don't always understand. It is filled with surprises and seems to hurry by before we have remembered to thank God for all that time has brought us. Peoples of the world have traditionally celebrated Midsummer Eve, the evening before the solstice, with rituals

using water and fire. Christians link this festival to the birth of John the Baptist, whose feast day is June 24, six months before the birth of Jesus.

The Christian calendar is rooted in nature's year, with its recurring cycle of heat and cold, rain and drought, growth and decline. Linked to those cycles are memories of events that remind us of our God who works with us in historical time. We remember the life and work of Christ, and also the life of the church. We turn the pages of the calendar like the pages of a family album, showing us first one saint or hero and then another. These are our ancestors in the work of redemption, a work that is still going on. Their stories are food for reflection. Here is John the Baptist (June 23 and 24): Is there anyone like him today? Here are first-century martyrs (June 30), and more recent martyrs of Uganda (June 3) and England (June 22): Where are people speaking out boldly for Christ today? Here are monks and poets and apostles. Here are men and women of many traditions. Each has something to teach us.

A PSALM FOR JUNE

PSALM 104:1–2, 13–15

▶ all make
the sign
of the cross

LEADER Bless the Lord, O my soul!
   ALL **O Lord my God, you are very great!**

LEADER You are clothed with honor and majesty,
and wrapped in light as with a garment.
From your lofty dwelling you water the mountains;
the earth is satisfied with the fruit of your work.
   ALL **Bless the Lord, O my soul!**
O Lord my God, you are very great!

LEADER You cause the grass to grow for cattle,
and plants for people to use,
to bring forth food from the earth,
wine to gladden the human heart,
oil to make the face shine,
and bread to strengthen the human heart.
   ALL **Bless the Lord, O my soul!**
O Lord my God, you are very great!

LEADER Glory to the Father, and to the Son,
and to the Holy Spirit:
as it was in the beginning, is now,
and will be for ever. Amen. Alleluia.
   ALL **Bless the Lord, O my soul!**
O Lord my God, you are very great!

▶ turn back to
Daily Prayer
for today

■ INTRODUCTION

Today is the memorial of Saint Justin, who died for his faith about the year 165. Justin was a philosopher *(fi-LAHS-ah-fer)*. This word means "one who loves wisdom." Philosophers think about the meaning of the universe, and about how all things work together. When Justin began to study Christianity, at first he thought that it was just another way of looking at life. Soon he saw that it was much more. It is a share in God's own wisdom.

■ A PSALM FOR JUNE

turn to
page 15

■ READING

Wisdom 6:12–16

Listen to the words of the book of Wisdom.

Wisdom shines brightly, and she is easily seen by all who love her and search for her.

Wisdom hurries to meet everyone who wants to be wise. If you get up early and search, you will easily find her at your front door.

Keep your mind on Wisdom, and you will be very wise. Keep thinking about her, and all of your worries will soon disappear.

Wisdom goes around searching for those who deserve her. She meets them along the road and stays in their thoughts.

The word of the Lord.

■ REFLECTION

How can I become more wise this summer? What wise people do I know? What has God already taught me about the meaning of life?

■ CLOSING

Let us remember these intentions:

Lord God,
   your wisdom led Saint Justin
   to study the meaning of life.
Share your wisdom with all your people.
Teach us your ways.
Brighten this earth with your presence,
   so that we may say with all the saints:
How lovely is your dwelling place,
   O Lord of hosts!
We ask this through Christ our Lord. **Amen.**

Let us pray with the words that Jesus taught us.

Our Father . . .

sing
"alleluia"

On this day in 1968 Helen Keller died. She was a woman who did not let her handicaps hold her back. Find her story in the library, or watch a video of *The Miracle Worker* today.

JUNE 2

■ INTRODUCTION

Today we remember Saint Elmo, a patron of sailors. This holy bishop died in Italy during the fourth century. The church where he is buried looks out over a great harbor where ships from all over the world, including the United States, are at anchor.

Let us pray for the safety of all who will be sailing this summer, and who will learn of God from the oceans, lakes and stars.

■ A PSALM FOR JUNE

 turn to page 15

■ READING

Psalm 107:23–26, 28–30

Listen to a reading from the book of Psalms.

Some went down to the sea in ships,
working on the mighty waters;
they saw the deeds of the Lord,
God's wondrous works in the deep.
For God commanded
    and raised the stormy wind,
which lifted up the waves of the sea.
The sailors mounted up to heaven,
they went down to the depths;
their courage melted away in their calamity.

Then they cried to the Lord in their trouble,
and God brought them out of their distress,
    made the storm be still,
and the waves of the sea were hushed.
Then they were glad because they had quiet,
and God brought them to their desired harbor.

The word of the Lord.

■ REFLECTION

How has God brought me to the port where I wanted to go? When was I in a storm and asked God to rescue me?

The word of the Lord.

■ CLOSING

Let us remember these intentions:

Loving God,
    we seek you in the wind,
    and find you in the storm.
We call to you in faith,
    and trust you in danger.
Be with us always,
    when we sail on troubled waters.
We ask this through Christ our Lord. **Amen.**

Let us pray with the words that Jesus taught us:

Our Father . . .

 sing "alleluia"

Sailors also ask the protection of Mary, the Mother of God. They call her "Maris Stella," which means Star of the Sea.

■ INTRODUCTION

Today is the memorial of Charles Lwanga *(luh-WANG-uh)* and 45 other Christian men and boys who died for their faith between 1886 and 1887. They worked for the king of Uganda *(you-GON-duh)* in Africa. The king hated their Christian faith. Their suffering was very cruel. Those who died were many different kinds of Christians: Catholics, Anglicans and Protestants. One of the martyrs said to his brother, "A well that has many sources never runs dry. When we are gone, others will come after us."

Hold the churches of Africa in your heart today. There is great faith there, and in some places, great suffering.

■ A PSALM FOR JUNE

turn to page 15

■ READING

Matthew 10:26–28, 29–31

Listen to the words of the holy gospel according to Matthew.

Jesus said to his disciples: "Don't be afraid of anyone! Everything that is hidden will be found out, and every secret will be known. Whatever I say to you in the dark, you must tell in the light. And you must announce from the housetops whatever I have whispered to you. Don't be afraid of people. They can kill you, but they cannot harm your soul.

"Aren't two sparrows sold for only a penny? But your father knows when any one of them falls to the ground. Even the hairs on your head are counted. So don't be afraid! You are worth much more than many sparrows."

The gospel of the Lord.

■ REFLECTION

What things should disciples of Jesus speak up about? What difficulties have I put up with for the sake of Jesus? What things am I afraid of?

■ CLOSING

Let us remember these intentions:

God our Protector,
     strengthen us with your grace,
     accept us as your disciples,
     and grant that all our words and works
     may be worthy of you,
     our holy and loving God.
We ask this through Christ our Lord. **Amen.**

Let us pray with the words that Jesus taught us.

Our Father . . .

sing "alleluia"

Open a window today in honor of Pope John XXIII (the twenty-third), who called a great council of all the bishops. He said it was a way to open the windows of the church and let in fresh air. He died June 3, 1963.

JUNE 4

INTRODUCTION

There are no major saints on the church's calendar for today, so remember the patron saints of your own family. You might write those names in the margins of this book and decorate them with joyful colors. Find the story of your saint and share it with someone.

The Hebrew people placed great importance on being able to call a person by name. They knew that naming is a holy act. The Bible is filled with stories of people who were named by God. Today's reading is one example.

A PSALM FOR JUNE

 turn to
page 15

READING

Genesis 32:24–28, 29–30

Listen to the words of the book of Genesis (JEN-*uh-sis*).

A man came and fought with Jacob until just before daybreak. When the man saw that he could not win, he struck Jacob on the hip and threw it out of joint. They kept on wrestling until the man said, "Let go of me! It's almost daylight."

"You can't go until you bless me," Jacob replied.

Then the man asked, "What is your name?"

"Jacob," he answered.

The man said, "Your name will no longer be Jacob. You have wrestled with God and with men, and you have won. That's why your name will be Israel." And he blessed Jacob.

Jacob said, "I have seen God face to face, and I am still alive."

The word of the Lord.

REFLECTION

Am I respectful of other people and their names? Do I show respect for the names of God? Do I ask the saints, living and dead, to pray for me?

CLOSING

Let us remember these intentions:

Loving God, bless each of us "whom you have fearfully and wonderfully made."

 name the members of your family
and the friends you want to remember

Bless and keep us all this day.
We ask this through Christ our Lord. **Amen.**

Let us pray with the words that Jesus taught us:

Our Father . . .

 sing
"alleluia"

Why were you given the name you have? Think about the importance of pen names or brand names. Why do we get upset when someone mispronounces our name, or by name-calling? Why is it insulting to call someone "what's-his-name" or "what's-her-name"?

19

JUNE 5

■ INTRODUCTION

Today we remember Saint Boniface *(BAHN-ah-fis)*, an English priest whose name means "speaker of Good News." In the year 722, he set out to bring the word of God to the German peoples. For 32 years he traveled in what is now Germany, France and Holland. His preaching brought thousands of people to be baptized. He opened schools and churches. He worked with kings to bring peace. It is said that he changed Europe more than any other Englishman.

■ A PSALM FOR JUNE

turn to
page 15

■ READING

Isaiah 52:7–10

Listen to the words of the prophet Isaiah *(eye-ZAY-uh)*.

What a beautiful sight!
On the mountains a messenger announces
    to Jerusalem *(juh-ROO-suh-lem)*,
"Good news! You are saved.
There will be peace.
    Your God is now King."
Everyone on guard duty, sing and celebrate!
Look! You can see the LORD returning to Zion.
Jerusalem, rise from the ruins!
    Join in the singing.
The LORD has given comfort to his people.
    He comes to your rescue.
The LORD has shown all nations
    his mighty strength.

Now everyone will see
    the saving power of our God.
The word of the Lord.

■ REFLECTION

Who are messengers of the good news in my town? Am I as excited as Isaiah and Boniface about God's kingdom coming among us? Do "join in the singing" in church?

■ CLOSING

Let us remember these intentions:

O God, through your living Word,
    strengthen those who believe,
      speak to those who listen,
    protect those who proclaim your gospel,
    and be with all those who bring
      your good news
      to the far corners of the world.
We ask this through Christ our Lord. **Amen.**

Let us pray with the words that Jesus taught us

Our Father . . .

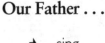
sing
"alleluia"

A legend tells us that Boniface used the beautiful evergreen trees of Germany as a symbol of God's everlasting life. So people began to decorate them at Christmas. Decorate an evergreen tree with a ribbon today in honor of Saint Boniface.

JUNE 6

INTRODUCTION

Today we remember Norbert, a holy bishop who died in 1134. Norbert did not start his life well. He spent too much time spending money and seeking pleasure. One day, Norbert was out riding and a thunderstorm frightened his horse. The horse threw him to the ground and he hit his head on a rock. When Norbert woke up he said, "Lord, what do you want me to do?" He heard an inner voice say, "Turn away from evil, and do good. Seek peace, and pursue it." From that moment, Norbert was a new man.

A PSALM FOR JUNE

 turn to page 15

READING

Matthew 9:10–13

Listen to the words of the holy gospel according to Matthew.

Jesus and his disciples were having dinner at Matthew's house. Many tax collectors and other sinners were also there. Some Pharisees asked Jesus' disciples, "Why does your teacher eat with tax collectors and other sinners?"

Jesus heard them and answered, "Healthy people don't need a doctor, but sick people do. Go and learn what the scriptures mean when they say, 'Instead of offering sacrifices to me, I want you to be merciful to others.' I didn't come to invite good people to be my followers. I came to invite sinners."

The gospel of the Lord.

REFLECTION

Why is it good for us that Jesus welcomes sinners? Can I be more "merciful to others"? How? Do I ever pray this prayer: "Lord, what do you want me to do?"

CLOSING

Let us remember these intentions:

Loving God,
>   you forgive us with all your heart
>   for the wrong we do.
Help us to forgive those who wrong us.
Help us to make peace in our families
>   and our neighborhoods.
We ask this through Christ our Lord. **Amen.**

Let us pray with the words that Jesus taught us:

Our Father . . .

 sing "alleluia"

On this day in 1944 the Allied Army landed on the beaches of Normandy in France. They had come to fight the Nazis (NOT-sees), who were trying to take over all the countries of Europe. Many thousands of soldiers died that day and during the months that followed, but eventually they were able to restore freedom and peace. This happened during the Second World War. Pray today for world peace.

■ INTRODUCTION

On this day in 632, an Arab prophet died. His name was Mohammed *(mo-HAH-med)*. He was a powerful preacher who helped people believe in the one true God. Mohammed taught that believers must surrender to the will of God. In Arabic, the word "surrender" is islam *(iss-LAHM)*. There are now over 900 million followers of Islam around the world. These people are called Muslims.

■ A PSALM FOR JUNE

 turn to page 15

■ READING

Wisdom 12:13, 16–19

Listen to the words of the book of Wisdom.

There is no God but you, and you care for all of us. You don't have to prove that you judge fairly. Your strength gives you the power to do right, and because you rule over all, you have pity on everyone.

When someone doubts how strong you are, you show your strength. And you correct everyone who is too proud. You are a powerful Master. But you judge us with kindness and rule with great mercy, because you have the power to do whatever you want.

By doing such things, you have taught your people that those who do right must also care about others. And you have given your children a wonderful hope by helping them turn from sin.

The word of the Lord.

■ REFLECTION

Muslim people pray five times each day. Do pray each day? Many Muslim women follow the custom of covering their heads with scarve Do I respect other people's customs and beliefs

■ CLOSING

Let us remember these intentions:

God most gracious and merciful,
    through the prophets you teach us
    to worship you alone,
    to treat others justly,
    and to care for the poor
Bless the Muslim people and grant them peace
Make them secure in their homes
    around the world, now and for ever. **Amen.**

Let us pray with the words that Jesus taught us

Our Father . . .

 sing "alleluia"

On this day in 1866 Chief Seattle died, sad that mar people failed to respect the earth. He said, "Every shinir pine needle, every sandy shore, every mist in the dar woods, every clearing and humming insect is holy in th memory and experience of my people. . . . We are pa of the earth and it is part of us." Do something kind fc the earth today.

JUNE 8

■ INTRODUCTION

Today we remember Gerard Manley Hopkins. He was studying at Oxford University in 1866 when he decided to become a Catholic. It was a hard decision because at that time Catholics were not allowed at Oxford, so Gerard had to leave. Many people knew that he was an excellent poet, but he gave that up too, in order to become a priest. After ten years he took up his pen again and wrote some of the finest religious poetry in the English language. He often wrote of the way the ordinary things of nature give praise to God. He wrote:

The world is charged
    with the grandeur of God.
It will flame out like shining from shook foil.

God's Grandeur

■ A PSALM FOR JUNE

 turn to page 15

■ READING

Isaiah 55:10–11

Listen to the words of the prophet Isaiah.

The rain and the snow fall from the sky.
But they don't return without watering the earth
    that produces seeds to plant and grain to eat.
And that is how it is with my words.
They don't return to me
    without doing everything I send them to do.
The word of the Lord.

■ REFLECTION

Both Father Hopkins and the prophet Isaiah learned about God from studying nature. What have I learned about God from the natural world? Do I speak to God when I am outdoors?

■ CLOSING

Let us remember these intentions:

Blessed are you, Lord our God,
    creator of the universe,
        you fill the world with your glory,
        and give it to us as a home.
Teach us to recognize its wonders,
        to treasure its variety,
        and to protect its fragile beauty.
We ask this through Christ our Lord. **Amen.**

Let us pray with the words that Jesus taught us:

Our Father . . .

 sing "alleluia"

After dark, go outside and think of Father Hopkins' words:
"Look at the stars! Look, look up at the skies!
O look at all the fire-folk sitting in the air!"

The Starlight Night

JUNE 9

■ INTRODUCTION

Today we remember Saint Ephrem *(EF-rum)*. He was a deacon of the church in Syria. The Syrians call him the "harp of the Holy Spirit" because of the beautiful poems, hymns and homilies that he wrote. After he retired from preaching, he spent his time praying and caring for the poor. Ephrem wore himself out caring for the sick during an epidemic, and died in 373.

Like Ephrem, write some poems about God today. It is a good way to welcome the summer, when the world around us is God's poem.

■ A PSALM FOR JUNE

➤ turn to page 15

■ READING

Matthew 13:3–9

Listen to the words of the holy gospel according to Matthew.

Jesus said: "A farmer went out to scatter seed in a field. While the farmer was scattering the seed, some of it fell along the road and was eaten by birds. Other seeds fell on thin, rocky ground and quickly started growing because the soil was not very deep. But when the sun came up, the plants were scorched and dried up, because they did not have enough roots.

"Some other seeds fell where thorn bushes grew up and choked the plants. But a few seeds did fall on good ground where the plants produced a hundred or sixty or thirty times as much as was scattered.

"If you have ears, pay attention!"

The gospel of the Lord.

■ REFLECTION

Jesus used nature to teach many things about God's ways. What can his story of the farmer teach me? If my heart is a field, what could be the seeds? the thorn bushes?

■ CLOSING

Let us remember these intentions:

Lord our God,
   fill our hearts with the seed of your word.
Help it to grow in us.
Teach us to receive your word with respect,
      to think it over carefully,
      and to follow it joyfully.
We ask this through Christ our Lord. **Amen.**

Let us pray with the words that Jesus taught us.

Our Father . . .

 sing "alleluia"

On this day in 1870, Charles Dickens died. He wrote many fine stories which you may know, such as *A Christmas Carol* and *Oliver Twist.* You may want to take one of his books out of the library. Some have been made into movies. See if the library has them on video.

JUNE 10

■ INTRODUCTION

On this day in 1935, William Wilson and Robert Smith founded Alcoholics Anonymous *(al-kuh-HOL-iks uh-NAH-nuh-mus),* or AA for short. Members of AA are addicted to alcohol or other drugs. They know that they cannot be healed without God's help. They meet regularly to encourage one another.

■ A PSALM FOR JUNE

turn to page 15

■ READING

Luke 7:11–16

Listen to the words of the holy gospel according to Luke.

Jesus and his disciples were on their way to the town of Nain *(NAY-in),* and a big crowd was going along with them. As they came near the gate of the town, they saw people carrying out the body of a widow's only son. Many people from the town were walking along with her.

When the Lord saw the woman, he felt sorry for her and said, "Don't cry!" Jesus went over and touched the stretcher on which the people were carrying the dead boy. They stopped, and Jesus said, "Young man, get up!" The boy sat up and began to speak. Jesus then gave him back to his mother.

Everyone was frightened and praised God. They said, "A great prophet is here with us! God has come to his people."

The gospel of the Lord.

■ REFLECTION

In the time of Jesus, women could not live without a man in the household. Jesus restored the widow's home life when he gave life to her son, because she had no one else with whom to live. How does the church help the homeless and lonely today? How does my family help? What does my family do to comfort people who have had a death in their family?

■ CLOSING

Let us remember these intentions:

Kind and merciful God,
    strengthen those who want to become sober.
Give them wise guides,
    loving friends,
    and success in their struggle.
Teach us to enjoy the freedom of your Spirit.
We ask this through Christ our Lord. **Amen.**

Let us pray with the words that Jesus taught us:

Our Father . . .

sing "alleluia"

National Little League Baseball Week begins on the second Monday of June. It reminds us to sign up for some sports this summer. It is a good way to have fun and make new friends, and it's good for our health too. Remember to thank all the adults and older students who organize the teams, do the coaching, and supply uniforms and equipment. Enjoy God's sunshine with your friends, and may the best team win!

JUNE 11

■ INTRODUCTION

Today we remember Saint Barnabas *(BAR-nuh-bus),* whose name means "man of encouragement." The Bible tells us that when Barnabas became a Christian, he sold his property and gave the money to the church. He became a teacher and a leader, and was sent to Antioch *(AN-tee-ock)* to guide the church there. Antioch is the city where the followers of Jesus were first called Christians.

Saint Barnabas asked Saint Paul to be his assistant, and for many years they traveled and taught together. They must have been good friends who worked well together. They are both called apostles by Saint Luke, although they were not among the twelve who followed Jesus before his death.

■ A PSALM FOR JUNE

turn to
page 15

■ READING

Acts 11:20–24

Listen to the words of the Acts of the Apostles.

Some of the followers went to Antioch and started telling Gentiles *(JEN-tilez)* the good news about the Lord Jesus. The Lord's power was with them, and many people turned to the Lord and put their faith in him. News of what was happening reached the church in Jerusalem. Then they sent Barnabas to Antioch.

When Barnabas got there and saw what God had been kind enough to do for them, he was very glad. So he begged them to remain faithful to the Lord with all their hearts. Barnabas was a good man of great faith, and he was fille with the Holy Spirit. Many more people turne to the Lord.

The word of the Lord.

■ REFLECTION

Who are some people I know who have "gre faith" and are "filled with the Holy Spirit" Barnabas was known as one who encourag others. What would I like to be known for?

■ CLOSING

Let us remember these intentions:

Lord God, we thank you for sending apostles to the whole world.
We welcome those who bring your good news
We pray for them and listen to their teaching.
Call on us, one day, to become apostles too.
We ask this through Christ our Lord. **Amen.**

Let us pray with the words that Jesus taught u

Our Father . . .

sing
"alleluia"

Today is King Kamehameha *(kuh-MAY-ha-MAY-ha)* Day Hawaii. In honor of the king who united the islands Hawaii, make a necklace of flowers and wear it. Also p the ukelele *(YOU-kuh-LAY-lee).* Do you know what ukelele is?

26

JUNE 12

INTRODUCTION

On this day in 1929, Anne Frank was born in Holland. When she was thirteen, during World War II, Anne and her family hid in a small attic because the Nazis wanted to capture all the Jewish people and kill them. After two years, they were discovered and sent to prison. Anne and most of her family were killed there.

During her time in the attic, Anne's dearest friend was her diary. In it, she wrote, "The best remedy for those who are afraid, lonely, or unhappy is to go outside, somewhere where they can be alone with the heavens, nature, and God. Because only then does one feel that all is as it should be and that God wishes to see people happy, amidst the simple beauty of nature."

A PSALM FOR JUNE

turn to page 15

READING

Jeremiah 20:10–12, 13

Listen to the words of the prophet Jeremiah (Jer-uh-MY-uh).

All of my friends are waiting for me to make a mistake. They say, "He will slip up. Then we can trap him and get even at last." But the LORD is with me like a mighty soldier. And those troublemakers will stumble, then fall down and fail. They will be forever disgraced and terribly ashamed.

LORD All-Powerful, you test everyone who does right, and you know everything anyone thinks or feels.

Sing and praise the LORD! He rescues the helpless from cruel oppressors.

The word of the Lord.

REFLECTION

Is there hatred or prejudice in my heart against anyone? Do I put people down? Do I pray for respect and cooperation among all peoples?

CLOSING

Let us remember these intentions:

Merciful God,
You rescue the helpless from cruel oppressors.
    and comfort all who are injured.
You know everything we think or feel.
Help us to love all people,
    and to protect those
    who are treated unkindly.
We ask this through Christ our Lord. **Amen.**

Let us pray with the words that Jesus taught us:

Our Father . . .

sing "alleluia"

Spend some time this summer putting your thoughts into a diary or journal. Read *The Diary of Anne Frank* for inspiration. Anne wrote, "I want to write, but more than that, I want to bring out all kinds of things that lie buried deep in my heart."

■ INTRODUCTION

Today we remember Saint Anthony, who was born about 800 years ago in Portugal. He was already a priest when he met some followers of Saint Francis. He saw how holy they were, so he too became a Franciscan. No one paid much attention to Anthony until the day he was asked to preach. He was so good at it that soon he was asked to give all his time to preaching.

Anthony's preaching brought reform to the city of Padua in Italy. He turned people from sinful lives, converted unbelievers, and worked to bring justice to the poor. Today Saint Anthony of Padua is honored as a patron of the poor. He is also said to help find lost articles— perhaps because he was able to find so many of God's lost sheep!

■ A PSALM FOR JUNE

turn to
page 15

■ READING

Proverbs 3:5–8, 11–12

Listen to the words of the book of Proverbs.

With all your heart you must trust the LORD
and not your own judgment.
Always let him lead you,
and he will clear the road
for you to follow.
Don't ever think that you are wise enough,
but respect the LORD
and stay away from evil.
This will make you healthy,
and you will feel strong.

My child, don't turn away or become bitter
when the LORD corrects you.
The LORD corrects everyone he loves,
just as parents correct their favorite child.

The word of the Lord.

■ REFLECTION

What kinds of health and strength come from trusting God? When my parents correct me, do I try to understand why?

■ CLOSING

Let us remember these intentions:

O God,
at your bidding the seed will sprout
and the shoot grow tall.
Teach us to trust in your ways,
to pray with confidence
and to follow your teachings
that we may abide forever in your kingdom.
We ask this through Christ our Lord. **Amen.**

Let us pray with the words that Jesus taught us

Our Father . . .

sing
"alleluia"

Saint Anthony is also the patron of those who cannot read. If you have trouble reading, ask for his help.

JUNE 14

INTRODUCTION

Today we remember Saint Basil, who grew up in a remarkable family. His grandmother, his parents, his brothers and his sister Macrina (July 19) were all named saints. Basil became a monk and made his monastery a center of care for the poor. He built a guest house, an orphanage and a school. He became a fine theologian, and his preaching led many people to live according to the gospel. He became a bishop, as famous in the fourth century as Pope John Paul is today. Even so, famous as he was, he put on his apron and helped to serve food to hungry people who came to him.

Basil was a man of many talents, yet he is most often remembered as a bishop who never stopped reminding his people with strong words that Christ asked them to share whatever they had with those in need. Basil's feast day is now January 2 where we honor him along with another great bishop named Gregory, who was Basil's good friend.

A PSALM FOR JUNE

turn to page 15

READING

2 Corinthians 9:7, 8, 10–11

Listen to the words of the apostle Paul.

Each of you must make up your own mind about how much to give. God loves people who love to give. God can bless you with everything you need, and you will always have more than enough to do all kinds of good things for others.

God gives seed to farmers and provides everyone with food. He will increase what you have, so that you can give even more to those in need. You will be blessed in every way, and you will be able to keep on being generous.

The word of the Lord.

REFLECTION

Is it time to begin the habit of giving a portion of my spending money to those who have a greater need? What else do I have that I can share with others? How can I serve others who need help?

CLOSING

Let us remember these intentions:

Just and loving God,
   open our eyes to the needs of others.
Show us your face when we look at them,
   so that our works and our words
   may be worthy of your kingdom.
We ask this through Christ our Lord. **Amen.**

Let us pray with the words that Jesus taught us:

Our Father . . .

sing "alleluia"

Flag Day! On this day in 1777, John Adams introduced a resolution to the Continental Congress: "that the flag of the thirteen United States shall be thirteen stripes, alternate red and white; that the union be thirteen stars, white on a blue field, representing a new constellation."

■ INTRODUCTION

Today we remember Saint Germaine Cousin, who was physically handicapped. Her father and stepmother made her sleep under the stairs, away from the other children, and work hard on the farm. Yet this real-life Cinderella remained cheerful, and shared with beggars the little food she was given. She died in 1602 at the age of 22.

■ A PSALM FOR JUNE

▶ turn to page 15

■ READING

Matthew 25:31, 32, 34–40

Listen to the words of the holy gospel according to Matthew.

Jesus said, "When the Son of Man comes in his glory with all of his angels, the people of all nations will be brought before him, and he will separate them, as shepherds separate their sheep from their goats. Then the king will say to those on his right, 'My father has blessed you! Come and receive the kingdom that was prepared for you before the world was created. When I was hungry, you gave me something to eat, and when I was thirsty, you gave me something to drink. When I was a stranger, you welcomed me, and when I was naked, you gave me clothes to wear. When I was sick, you took care of me, and when I was in jail, you visited me.'

"Then the ones who pleased the Lord will ask, 'When did we give you something to eat or drink? When did we welcome you as a stranger or give you clothes to wear or visit you whil you were sick or in jail?' The king will answe 'Whenever you did it for any of my people, n matter how unimportant they seemed, you did for me.'"

The gospel of the Lord.

■ REFLECTION

What have I shared? Whom have I visited Have I cheered anyone up? Is there someon who needs my help?

■ CLOSING

Let us remember these intentions:

Just and loving God,
    open our eyes to the needs of others.
Show us your face when we look at them,
    so that our works and our words
    may be worthy of your kingdom.
We ask this through Christ our Lord. **Amen.**

Let us pray with the words that Jesus taught us

Our Father . . .

▶ sing "alleluia"

On this day in 1215, King John of England signed th Magna Carta, a "bill of rights" setting limits to the pow of rulers. Read the United States Bill of Rights (the fir ten amendments to the Constitution).

JUNE 16

INTRODUCTION

On this day in 1987, the last dusky seaside sparrow died. This bird was named "Orange Band," and it died in a cage at Walt Disney World. This kind of bird had lived in the wetlands on the coast of Florida. Now there are no more of them, forever!

This is a good day to pray for all the creatures of this earth, especially those that are endangered. And let us make a commitment not to harm or tease any of God's creatures.

A PSALM FOR JUNE

 turn to
page 15

READING

Wisdom 1:12–15, 2:23–24

Listen to the words of the book of Wisdom.

Do not invite death by the error of your life,
    or bring on destruction by the works
        of your hands.
God did not create death, and he is sad
    whenever a living creature dies.
God made everything,
    and there is a reason for every living creature.
No deadly poison is in them,
    and the kingdom of death
        doesn't rule the earth.
Goodness will never die.
God created us to live forever, just as he does.
But the Devil was jealous
    and brought death into the world.

The word of the Lord.

REFLECTION

How can my family help protect endangered creatures? How can we be more careful of the earth? Do we reduce, reuse, and recycle?

CLOSING

Let us remember these intentions:

Blessed are you, Lord our God,
    creator of the universe,
        you give us the world as a home,
        and fill it with your glory.
Teach us to recognize the wonders of the earth,
    to treasure its variety,
        and to protect its fragile beauty.
We ask this through Christ our Lord. **Amen.**

Let us pray with the words that Jesus taught us:

Our Father . . .

 sing
"alleluia"

A puzzle: In a speech on this day in 1858, Abraham Lincoln quoted Mark 3:25: "a house divided against itself cannot stand." What house was he talking about?

■ INTRODUCTION

On this day in 1703, John Wesley was born. As a student, John started a Bible study group. He and his group were so religious the other students mockingly called them "Methodists."

John was ordained and came as a missionary to Georgia, where he taught the people that they should be loving toward one another. He wrote, "May we not be of one heart, though we are not of one opinion?"

■ A PSALM FOR JUNE

 turn to page 15

■ READING

Ephesians 4:1–6

Listen to the words of the apostle Paul.

Brothers and sisters:
As a prisoner of the Lord, I beg you to live in a way that is worthy of the people God has chosen to be his own. Always be humble and gentle. Patiently put up with each other and love each other. Try your best to let God's Spirit keep your hearts united. Do this by living at peace.

All of you are part of the same body. There is only one Spirit of God, just as you were given one hope when you were chosen to be God's people.

We have only one Lord, one faith, and one baptism. There is one God who is the Father of all people. Not only is God above all others, but God works by using all of us, and God lives in all of us.

The word of the Lord.

■ REFLECTION

Is there a Methodist church in my neighborhood? Do members of my parish work with Methodists on any projects? Do I remember to pray for the unity of all Christians?

■ CLOSING

Let us remember these intentions:

God of all nations and Creator of all peoples,
   you call us to be worthy disciples of Jesus.
Guide all Christians to live together in peace
   in this neighborhood,
   in this nation,
   and on this planet.
We ask this through Christ our Lord. **Amen.**

Let us pray with the words that Jesus taught us

Our Father . . .

 sing "alleluia"

There are nine groups of Methodist churches in the United States. They have more than 14 million members. Methodists are known for their hymns and for their care of the poor. (*World Almanac*)

JUNE 18

∎ INTRODUCTION

On this day in 1872, Susan B. Anthony was convicted in a New York court of a crime: trying to vote. She was challenging laws that denied women rights that belong to all citizens. Now all citizens are able to vote. But we still work for the day when everyone has an equal chance for jobs, education and other opportunities.

On this day in 1983, Sally Ride, a scientist and a pilot, became the first American woman in space. Susan B. Anthony would be proud to know that a woman of courage served her country as an astronaut.

∎ A PSALM FOR JUNE

turn to
page 15

∎ READING

Matthew 13:44–46

Listen to the words of the holy gospel according to Matthew.

Jesus said to his disciples: "The kingdom of heaven is like what happens when someone finds treasure hidden in a field and buries it again. A person like that is happy and goes and sells everything in order to buy that field.

"The kingdom of heaven is like what happens when a shop owner is looking for fine pearls. After finding a very valuable one, the owner goes and sells everything in order to buy that pearl."

The gospel of the Lord.

∎ REFLECTION

What is worth more to me than anything else? How is faith like a hidden treasure or a valuable pearl? What have I given up because of something more important?

∎ CLOSING

Let us remember these intentions:

Lord God,
    you are the pearl we seek,
    the treasure we long for.
Show us what is important.
    that we may discover you
    in all that we do.
We ask this through Christ our Lord. Amen.

Let us pray with the words that Jesus taught us:

Our Father . . .

sing
"alleluia"

Today is a day to look up at the sky and dream of the challenges and adventures that your life will hold.

■ INTRODUCTION

Today we remember Saint Romuald *(ROE-moo-ald)*. He went to a monastery to pray for 40 days, and he liked it so much that he decided to stay there. He gave such full attention to God that he became wise and holy. People came from miles around to seek his guidance.

Like Romuald, the author of today's reading was a wise teacher.

■ A PSALM FOR JUNE

turn to page 15

■ READING

Ecclesiastes 12:9–10, 11, 12–14

Listen to the words of the book of Ecclesiastes *(ee-klee-zee-AST-eez)*.

I was a wise teacher with much understanding, and I collected a number of proverbs that I had carefully studied. Then I tried to explain these things in the best and most accurate way.

These sayings come from God, our only shepherd, and they are like nails that fasten things together.

There is no end to books,
and too much study will wear you out.

Everything you were taught can be put into a few words:

Respect and obey God!
This is what life is all about.
God will judge everything we do,
even what is done in secret,
whether good or bad.

The word of the Lord.

■ REFLECTION

Do I agree that "too much study will wear m out"? What are some summer ways of learning Do I know enough about the Bible to say son things from memory?

■ CLOSING

Let us remember these intentions:

God, our only shepherd,
do not let us stumble and fall.
With your wisdom guide us,
along with our family and friends,
our teachers, leaders and heroes.
And bring us one day
into your heavenly kingdom.
We ask this through Christ our Lord. **Amen.**

Let us pray with the words that Jesus taught u

Our Father . . .

sing "alleluia"

A proverb is a short, clever or poetic way of sayir something wise. It is easy to remember, such as: "Has makes waste," or "Beauty is only skin deep." This one from the Bible: "Having a lazy person on the job is like mouth full of vinegar or smoke in your eyes." Copy son proverbs in your diary. Write some of your own.

INTRODUCTION

e cannot let the month go by without asking
d to bless all of June's brides and grooms.
arriage is a holy and wonderful state. It is fit-
g that we celebrate the beginning of a marriage
th the gathered church and a lovely party.

When a couple marry they set out on an
venture together. They make plans to create a
me for their family, to raise and educate their
ildren, and to work for a just and happy neigh-
rhood and world. This is not easy, but love
akes them joyful and grace makes them gen-
us. Saint Paul reminds us that husbands and
ves love each other just as Jesus and the church
ve each other. When you see a happy bride and
oom, you are catching a glimpse of the excite-
ent and loving kindness of God's kingdom.

A PSALM FOR JUNE

 turn to
page 15

READING

Ephesians 5:1, 24–25, 31–33

sten to the words of the apostle Paul.

o as God does. After all, you are his dear
ildren. Let love be your guide.

Wives should always put their husbands first,
the church puts Christ first. A husband should
ve his wife as much as Christ loved the church
d gave his life for it.

As the Scriptures say, "A man leaves his father
d mother to get married, and he becomes like
e person with his wife." This is a great mys-
ry, but I understand it to mean Christ and his

church. So each husband should love his wife as
much as he loves himself, and each wife should
respect her husband.

The word of the Lord.

■ REFLECTION

What are some ways the married people I know
show their love and care for one another? Do I
know someone who is the kind of husband or
wife I want to be? Have I let TV shape my ideas
of what marriage is like?

■ CLOSING

Let us remember these intentions:

Loving God,
    as you unite Jesus and his church,
    bless and unite all who choose to marry.
Teach them love that is not afraid of sacrifice,
    friendship that rejoices in the other's good,
    and openness to the needs of the world.
We ask this through Christ our Lord. **Amen.**

Let us pray with the words that Jesus taught us:

Our Father . . .

 sing
"alleluia"

Look at wedding photos in your family album. Ask your
parents or relatives about their ideas of marriage, and
whether their ideas have changed over time. Make a
card and send it to someone who is having a wedding
or anniversary.

JUNE 21

■ INTRODUCTION

Some people pray only when they are in church, but others turn their hearts to God often during the day. Today we remember two saints who learned to do this when they were young. Blessed Osanna, who lived in the fifteenth century, was only five years old when she saw a vision of heaven. This happened as she was walking along the river. She was happy to know that God was with her everywhere she went.

Saint Aloysius Gonzaga *(al-oh-WISH-us gon-ZAG-uh)* lived about a hundred years later. He decided at the age of seven to begin each day by praying the psalms. He kept this habit all his life.

■ A PSALM FOR JUNE

turn to
page 15

■ READING

Luke 11:1–4

Listen to the words of the holy gospel according to Luke.

One of his disciples said to Jesus, "Lord, teach us to pray, just as John the Baptist taught his followers to pray."

So Jesus told them, "Pray in this way:
'Father, help us to honor your name.
Come and set up your kingdom.
Give us each day the food we need.
Forgive our sins, as we forgive everyone
    who has done wrong to us.
And keep us from being tempted.'"

The gospel of the Lord.

■ REFLECTION

Do I cooperate when my family prays togethe
Do I remember to pray when I am alone? Ho
well do I understand the prayer Jesus taught u

■ CLOSING

Let us remember these intentions:

Loving God,
    you call us each by name
    and speak to us in the quiet of our hearts.
Speak to us of love for all people.
Speak to us of hope for our world.
Speak to us of your gift of salvation.
Speak to us, for we are listening.
We ask this through Christ our Lord. **Amen.**

Let us pray with the words that Jesus taught u

Our Father . . .

sing
"alleluia"

This is the time of the summer solstice, when the nor
ern hemisphere is blessed with its greatest amount
sunlight. Christians save their celebration for the feast
Saint John the Baptist, on June 24. You have a few da
left to make plans!

JUNE 22

INTRODUCTION

today we remember Saint Thomas More, a talented and loyal advisor to King Henry VIII of England. When Henry wanted Thomas to obey him instead of the Catholic church, Thomas would not do it. The king took away Thomas' office and money, and turned many people against him. But Thomas wrote, "Reputation, honor, fame, what is all that but a breath of air from another person's mouth, no sooner spoken but gone? Whoever finds his delight in them is feeding on wind." Finally King Henry had Thomas executed.

This was the beginning of 150 years of religious wars in England, when many holy men and women died. Pray today for peace and respect among people of all faiths.

A PSALM FOR JUNE

turn to
page 15

READING

Matthew 16:24–25

Listen to the words of the holy gospel according to Matthew.

Jesus said to his disciples: "If any of you want to be my followers, you must forget about yourself. You must take up your cross and follow me. If you want to save your life, you will destroy it. But if you give up your life for me, you will find it."

The gospel of the Lord.

■ REFLECTION

How can worrying about myself keep me from following Jesus? Did Jesus mean that we should do dangerous things? Do my friends ever make it hard for me to do the right thing?

■ CLOSING

Let us remember these intentions:

Loving God,
    on the day of our baptism,
    you signed us with the cross of Christ,
    that we might live in its power.
Bless us with this sign of glory,
    and let it remind us that Jesus died
    and rose for all.
Help us to carry the cross with him,
    and to follow him each day in serving others.
We ask this through Christ our Lord. **Amen.**

Let us pray with the words that Jesus taught us:

Our Father . . .

sing
"alleluia"

Thomas More shares this feast day with Saint John Fisher, a brave bishop who also defied King Henry VIII. He, too, went to his death rather than betray his Catholic faith.

JUNE 23

■ INTRODUCTION

This is Midsummer Eve, a day to rejoice in the goodness and freedom of summer, the season of growth. Tonight is the eve of the Birth of Saint John the Baptist. John baptized with water, and he pointed to Jesus, the light of the world. So we use water and light in our celebrations.

In many places bonfires are lighted along the water's edge. In Canada, there are bonfires on both sides of the Saint Lawrence River. In San Juan *(hwan)*, Puerto Rico, which is named after Saint John, people swim in the cool sea after midnight to honor John the Baptist. Perhaps your family can celebrate with a splash, a cook-out, and a sing-along after dark.

■ A PSALM FOR JUNE

turn to page 15

■ READING

Luke 1:8, 11–15

Listen to the words of the holy gospel according to Luke.

One day Zechariah's *(zek-uh-RYE-uhz)* group of priests were on duty, and he was serving God as a priest.

All at once an angel from the Lord appeared to Zechariah at the right side of the altar. Zechariah was confused and afraid when he saw the angel. But the angel told him:

"Don't be afraid, Zechariah! God has heard your prayers. Your wife Elizabeth will have a son, and you must name him John. His birth will make you very happy, and many people

will be glad. Your son will be a great servant the Lord."

The gospel of the Lord.

■ REFLECTION

All birth, all life is precious to the Lord. D thank God for my life? Do I thank God for r baptism?

■ CLOSING

Let us remember these intentions:

Loving God,
  you raised up John the Baptist
  to prepare the way for the coming
    of your Son, Jesus.
Let us share with John and all your people
  the good news of your saving presence
We ask this through Christ our Lord. **Amen.**

Let us pray with the words that Jesus taught u

Our Father . . .

sing
"alleluia"

Some customs for the Birth of John the Baptist rem us of Christmas, which is exactly half a year away Poland, wreaths with lighted candles, like Advent wreat are floated on the streams and rivers.

INTRODUCTION

day we honor the birth of Saint John the
ptist, the prophet sent by God to prepare the
y for Jesus. We celebrate this feast six months
m Christmas Eve, because Luke's gospel tells
that John was born six months before Jesus,
o was his cousin.

John pointed out Jesus to his disciples, and he
d of him, "He must increase, I must decrease."
is makes midsummer the perfect time for
n's birthday. From now on the days grow
rter, while after the birthday of Jesus the days
w longer.

A PSALM FOR JUNE

turn to
page 15

READING

Luke 1:57–64

ten to the words of the holy gospel according
Luke.

en Elizabeth's son was born, her neighbors
d relatives heard how kind the Lord had been
her, and they too were glad.

Eight days later they did for the child what
Law of Moses commands. They were going
name him Zechariah, after his father. But
zabeth said, "No! His name is John."

The people argued, "No one in your family
ever been named John." So they motioned
Zechariah to find out what he wanted to
ne his son.

Zechariah asked for a writing tablet. Then
wrote, "His name is John." Everyone was
amazed. Right away Zechariah started speaking
and praising God.

The gospel of the Lord.

■ REFLECTION

After he learned that Elizabeth would give birth
to a son, Zechariah lost the power of speech.
Have I ever been left speechless by the wonders
of God? How do I use my voice in God's service? Do I sing with enthusiasm when I praise
God with others?

■ CLOSING

Let us remember these intentions:

Loving God,
    you raised up John the Baptist
    to prepare the way for the coming
        of your Son, Jesus.
Let us share with John and all your people
    the good news of your saving presence
We ask this through Christ our Lord. **Amen.**

Let us pray with the words that Jesus taught us:

Our Father . . .

sing
"alleluia"

Remember your own baptism as you celebrate the birth
of John the Baptist today. Ask your parents to tell you
about it if you were too young to remember it yourself.
Be thankful for the wonderful gift of baptism.

JUNE 25

■ INTRODUCTION

Today we remember Saint Eurosia *(you-RO-shuh)*, a Spanish martyr of the eighth century. Little is known about Eurosia except that her story and her devotion was carried by Spanish soldiers into Italy, where she is also honored. Eurosia is known as the protector of crops, and also as a saint to ask for help during bad weather.

You can bless your garden today, and ask Saint Eurosia to protect it. Remember the farms and gardens around the world in your prayer.

■ A PSALM FOR JUNE

turn to page 15

■ READING

John 6:5, 8-9, 11–12

Listen to the words of the holy gospel according to John.

When Jesus saw the large crowd coming toward him, he asked Philip, "Where will we get enough food to feed all these people?"

Andrew, the brother of Simon Peter, was one of the disciples. He spoke up and said, "There is a boy here who has five small loaves of barley bread and two fish. But what good is that with all these people?"

Jesus took the bread in his hands and gave thanks to God. Then he passed the bread to the people, and he did the same with the fish, until everyone had plenty to eat. The people ate all they wanted, and Jesus told his disciples to gather up the leftovers, so that nothing would be wasted.

The gospel of the Lord.

■ REFLECTION

How does Jesus feed his followers today? H[o]w does God feed the world? Why is it that so[me] people go hungry, or even starve to death? W[hat] do I do to help feed the hungry?

■ CLOSING

Let us remember these intentions:

God is the Ruler of all creation.
Let all that is living sing praise!
God's goodness fills the earth.
Let all that is living sing praise!
Green leaves and bright flowers, sing praise!
Waving wheat and ripening grapes, sing prais[e!]
Let all that is living sing praise!
We ask this through Christ our Lord. **Amen.**

Let us pray with the words that Jesus taught [us.]

Our Father . . .

sing "alleluia"

On this date in 1876 George Custer and 200 soldi[ers] were defeated near the Little Big Horn River in Monta[na]. Sioux and Cheyenne Indians led by chiefs Sitting Bull a[nd] Crazy Horse also lost that day, although they did n[ot] realize it until later. News of the battle brought more s[et]tlers and soldiers to the area, who eventually pushed [the] Native Americans off the land they loved.

40

JUNE 26

◼ INTRODUCTION

Today we remember Virgil Michel *(MY-kul)*, a monk who helped American Catholics learn more about the church's worship. In the 1920s, the Mass prayers were in the Latin language, and many people were happy just to watch and listen. Virgil knew that all of us are part of the body of Christ, not just the priests. The whole Christ celebrates the eucharist. The whole Christ welcomes new members through baptism.

Virgil Michel studied, taught and wrote articles. He began a magazine that is still published today. By the time he died in 1938, many Catholics were ready to take up his work.

◼ A PSALM FOR JUNE

turn to
page 15

◼ READING

I Corinthians 12: 12–13, 24–27

Listen to the words of the apostle Paul.

The body of Christ has many different parts, just as any other body does. Some of us are Jews, and others are Gentiles. Some of us are slaves, and others are free. But God's Spirit baptized each of us and made up part of the body of Christ. Now we each drink from that same Spirit.

God put our bodies together in such a way that even the parts that seem the least important are valuable. He did this to make all parts of the body work together smoothly, with each part caring about the others. If one part of our body hurts, we hurt all over. If one part of our body is honored, the whole body will be happy.

Together you are the body of Christ. Each one of you is part of his body.

The word of the Lord.

◼ REFLECTION

Do I truly participate in the Mass or do I just watch? Am I an active Christian all day long? Do I treat other people with the respect that I show to my own body, as if they were part of me?

◼ CLOSING

Let us remember these intentions:

Christ our Savior,
  we have been cared for and protected.
We have eaten and been filled.
Grant that, united with your church,
  and strengthened by your Spirit,
  we may be your worthy disciples,
  now and for ever. **Amen.**

Let us pray with the words that Jesus taught us:

Our Father . . .

sing
"alleluia"

On this day in 1945, the United Nations Charter was signed by the representatives of 50 nations. The UN is an assembly where all nations work for international justice and peace. Find out more about the UN today.

41

JUNE 27

■ INTRODUCTION

Today we remember Saint Cyril *(SEE-rul),* a bishop of Alexandria in Egypt. In the fifth century, Christians became confused about Jesus. They knew that he was the long-awaited savior sent by God. But some said that he was not truly God, just a very holy person. Others said that he was God in a body, but not truly human. People took sides. Bishops argued and exiled people and were having a terrible time.

The bishops decided to meet in the town of Ephesus *(EF-uh-sus).* Bishop Cyril was a strong leader, and he explained to the council of bishops that Jesus is both truly divine and truly human. We share our faith in this teaching when we call Mary the "Mother of God," or when we make the sign of the cross, naming God as Father, Son and Holy Spirit.

■ A PSALM FOR JUNE

turn to page 15

■ READING

Matthew 16:15–19

Listen to the words of the holy gospel according to Matthew.

Jesus asked the disciples, "Who do you say I am?"

Simon Peter spoke up, "You are the Messiah, the Son of the living God."

Jesus told him: "Simon, son of Jonah, you are blessed! You didn't discover this on your own. It was shown to you by my Father in heaven. So I will call you Peter, which means 'a rock.' On this rock I will build my church, and death itsel[f] will not have any power over it. I will give yo[u] the keys to the kingdom of heaven, and God i[n] heaven will allow whatever you allow on earth.

The gospel of the Lord.

■ REFLECTION

Why is it important that Jesus, our Messiah, i[s] God? Why is it important that Jesus is a huma[n] like us? Is my faith as solid as a rock?

■ CLOSING

Let us remember these intentions:

Gracious God,
  through the gift of your Spirit
  and the teaching of your apostles
  we can proclaim with all the church
  that Jesus is our Lord and Messiah.
Strengthen in us your gift of faith.
We ask this through Christ our Lord. **Amen.**

Let us pray with the words that Jesus taught us[.]

Our Father . . .

sing "alleluia"

Celebrate our Lord and Messiah by putting flowers o[r] bright fabric near a picture, crucifix or other image o[f] Jesus. Draw a picture or make a clay figure. Write [a] prayer. Sing a song.

INTRODUCTION

Today we remember Saint Irenaeus *(ee-rah-NAY-us),* who died around the year 203. His name means "peaceful one," and he did bring peace to many early Christian communities through his clear teaching.

Irenaeus traveled as a missionary to what is now France, and he became an assistant to the bishop of Lyon *(lee-OHN).* When the bishop was martyred, the members of the church elected Irenaeus to take his place. Irenaeus began to explain the meaning of the church, so that the other townspeople would not fear and persecute Christians. He also wanted Christians themselves to be clear about the teachings of the church. He was the first Christian teacher to write books about the meaning of the Bible. Irenaeus the peacemaker did not try to overcome his enemies with power, but with truth.

A PSALM FOR JUNE

turn to
page 15

READING

Romans 8:14–18

Listen to the words of the apostle Paul.

Brothers and sisters:

Only those people who are led by God's Spirit are God's children. God's Spirit doesn't make us slaves who are afraid. Instead, we become God's children and call God our Father. God's Spirit makes us sure that we are his children.

God's Spirit lets us know that together with Christ we will be given what God has promised.

We will also share in the glory of Christ, because we have suffered with him.

I am sure that what we are suffering now cannot compare with the glory that will be shown to us.

The word of the Lord.

■ REFLECTION

How does God's Spirit lead me? How might a person's slave act? How might a person's child act? How has God's glory been shown by artists or musicians?

■ CLOSING

Let us remember these intentions:

God of grace and wisdom,
    you continually raise up good people
    who show with their teachings
    that we follow a holy and loving God.
Let our lives be as true as our faith.
We ask this through Christ our Lord. **Amen.**

Let us pray with the words that Jesus taught us:

Our Father . . .

sing
"alleluia"

Celebrate belonging to God's family. Look at your family album. When you go to church on Sunday, look around at all the people who are your brothers and sisters. Give each person who lives in your house a hug.

■ INTRODUCTION

Today we remember Saints Peter and Paul. They shaped the church in its early years.

Peter was given his name by Jesus. His name means "rock" or "stone." This had great meaning to the people of Judea, who could look around and see solid rock formations on one side, and on the other, shifting sand dunes blown by every wind. In Peter Jesus gave the church a solid leader.

Paul first tried to stop the spread of the gospel by putting Christians into prison. Then, in a vision, he learned that Jesus is the Messiah, and those who harm his followers harm Jesus. Some of Paul's letters are in the Bible.

■ A PSALM FOR JUNE

turn to page 15

■ READING
John 21:15–17, 19

Listen to the words of the holy gospel according to John.

When Jesus and his disciples had finished eating, he asked, "Simon son of John, do you love me more than the others do?" Simon Peter answered, "Yes, Lord, you know I do!" "Then feed my lambs," Jesus said.

Jesus asked a second time, "Simon son of John, do you love me?" Peter answered, "Yes, Lord, you know I love you!" "Then take care of my sheep," Jesus told him.

Jesus asked a third time, "Simon son of John, do you love me?" Peter was hurt because Jesus had asked him three times if he loved him. So told Jesus, "Lord, you know everything. Y know I love you." Jesus replied, "Feed my sheep

Then he said to Peter, "Follow me!"

The gospel of the Lord.

■ REFLECTION

Who are Jesus' sheep and lambs? Catholi believe that the pope follows in the footsteps Peter. How does the pope feed God's peopl What do you know about the pope?

■ CLOSING

Let us remember these intentions:

Jesus our redeemer, we thank you
    for your apostles Peter and Paul,
    and for all holy bishops and teachers
    who serve your church.
Guide and protect them now and for ever.
    Amen.

Let us pray with the words that Jesus taught u

Our Father . . .

sing "alleluia"

According to legend, if you pray to Saints Peter and Pa on this day, you will be protected from snake bites f the whole year.

JUNE 30

INTRODUCTION

Yesterday we honored Saints Peter and Paul, who both died for their faith. Today we remember all the others who died during the same persecution. We call them the "First Martyrs of the Church of Rome."

In the summer of the year 64, a ten-day fire broke out in Rome. It wiped out two-thirds of the great city and left thousands of people dead, injured or homeless. Emperor Nero (NEE-ro) blamed the fire on the Christians. Christians were arrested, cruelly tortured and killed. The persecution went on for four years, until the death of Nero.

A PSALM FOR JUNE

turn to
page 15

READING

Mark 4:35–36, 37–41

Listen to the words of the holy gospel according to Mark.

Jesus said to his disciples, "Let's cross to the east side of the lake." So they left the crowd, and his disciples started across the lake with him in the boat. Suddenly a windstorm struck the lake. Waves started splashing into the boat, and it was about to sink. Jesus was in the back of the boat with his head on a pillow, and he was asleep. His disciples woke him and said, "Teacher, don't you care that we're about to drown?"

Jesus got up and ordered the wind and the waves to be quiet. The wind stopped, and everything was calm. Jesus asked his disciples, "Why were you afraid? Don't you have any faith?"

Now they were more afraid than ever and said to each other, "Who is this? Even the wind and the waves obey him!"

The gospel of the Lord.

REFLECTION

How were the early Christians caught in a storm? Have there been situations for me or for my family when we felt as though we were about to drown? What kind of faith does God ask of me today?

CLOSING

Let us remember these intentions:

Merciful God,
  you care for us with unchanging love.
Defend us against evil.
Make us brave and faithful,
  and strengthen us in times of suffering.
We ask this through Christ our Lord. **Amen.**

Let us pray with the words that Jesus taught us:

Our Father . . .

sing
"alleluia"

Are there any people you know who are worried? suffering? fearful? Send a card or letter to help cheer them up.

JULY

THE MONTH OF JULY

The seventh month of the year is named for the ancient Roman emperor Julius Caesar, who commanded his mathematicians to improve the calendar that was in use back then. The Romans got it almost right, and the Julian calendar was used for more than 16 centuries. Pope Gregory's mathematicians made some changes in 1582, but it was too late to name a month for him. But we do call his revision the Gregorian calendar, which is only fair.

During July we have some of the most beautiful weather of the year, which is why we spend so much time outside. To help us remember to thank God for the wonders of nature, this book sets aside a day to think about the earth (July 7) and water (July 10). This month is very important to the growth of crops and gardens, so if you want to pray about rain (too much or too little), Prayers about Rain are on page 6.

One of the most important days on our civil calendar is, of course, the Fourth of July. It is a day to pray about the freedoms that we enjoy in this nation and the heroes who have worked to protect those freedoms. We are never too young or too old to learn more about the work of building a just and peaceful nation.

Many other national days are celebrated in July. Our neighbor Canada as well as the African nations of Burundi and Rwanda celebrate their independence on July 1. The tiny island nation of Tonga shares July 4 with us. In fact, there are more than 23 independence days in July. Perhaps the beautiful weather makes people more determined to protect their freedom! Other anniversaries that are interesting for a freedom-loving people are the cracking of the Liberty Bell (July 8), and the birthdays of Nelson Mandela (July 18) and Simon Bolivar (July 24).

A number of biblical figures are remembered during July. They include Martha (July 29), Mary Magdalene (July 22), Aquila and Priscilla (July 8), and our apostles of the month, Thomas (July 3) and James (July 25). We also remember Joachim and Ann (July 26), and Veronica (July 12), though their names are not in the Bible. As always, there are saints from many historical periods and many nations. The church offers us wonderful stories to amaze and encourage us as we try to live each day as a disciple of the Lord.

A PSALM FOR JULY

[P]SALM 33:1, 13–14, 20–21

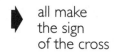

▶ all make
the sign
of the cross

LEADER Rejoice in the Lord!
 ALL **Sing to the Lord a new song!**

LEADER Let all the earth fear the Lord,
 let all the inhabitants of the world stand in awe!
 For the Lord spoke, and it came to be,
 the Lord commanded, and it stood forth.
 ALL **Rejoice in the Lord!**
 Sing to the Lord a new song!

LEADER The Lord looks down from heaven,
 and sees all people;
 the Lord sits enthroned and looks forth
 on all the inhabitants of the earth.
 ALL **Rejoice in the Lord!**
 Sing to the Lord a new song!

LEADER We wait for the Lord,
 who is our help and shield.
 Our heart is glad in the Lord,
 because we trust in God's holy name.
 ALL **Rejoice in the Lord!**
 Sing to the Lord a new song!

LEADER Glory to the Father, and to the Son,
 and to the Holy Spirit:
 as it was in the beginning, is now,
 and will be for ever. Amen. Alleluia.
 ALL **Rejoice in the Lord!**
 Sing to the Lord a new song!

▶ turn back to
Daily Prayer
for today

■ INTRODUCTION

Today we remember Blessed Junipero Serra *(you-NIH-per-oh SAY-ruh)*, a Franciscan who came to the Americas from Spain in 1748 as a teacher and missionary. He spent twenty years in Mexico, then went with explorers into what is now California. During the next fifteen years he built a string of missions, like rosary beads, along the Pacific coast, San Diego was the first one of the nine he started. Each mission was a day's walk from the next one. Some of the missions are now large cities. See if you can find some on a map.

At the missions, Native Americans were taught farming and other trades. But they were forced to speak Spanish and not their own languages, and were sometimes treated harshly. It is sad to know that the preaching of the gospel was sometimes accompanied by injustice.

■ A PSALM FOR JULY

turn to
page 49

■ READING

Mark 4:30–33

Listen to the words of the holy gospel according to Mark.

Jesus said: "What is God's kingdom like? What story can I use to explain it? It is like what happens when a mustard seed is planted in the ground. It is the smallest seed in all the world. But once it is planted, it grows larger than any garden plant. It even puts out branches that are big enough for birds to nest in its shade."

Jesus used many other stories when he spoke to the people, and he taught them as much as they could understand.

The gospel of the Lord.

■ REFLECTION

How was each of the Franciscan missions in California like a small seed? How has the kingdom of God sprouted in my life? What are signs that the church is growing?

■ CLOSING

Let us remember these intentions:

Lord God,
    fill our hearts with the seed of your word.
Help it to grow in us.
Teach us to receive your word with respect,
    to think it over carefully,
    and to follow it joyfully.
We ask this through Christ our Lord. **Amen.**

Let us pray with the words that Jesus taught us

Our Father . . .

sing
"alleluia"

This is Canada Day. Since 1867 Canada has been independent nation in the British Commonwealth. From now until July 4, a freedom festival is held on both sides of the Detroit River, where the United States and Canada meet.

JULY 2

INTRODUCTION

On this day in 1964, President Lyndon Johnson signed the Civil Rights Act. For many years African Americans had been segregated at restaurants, theaters, schools and churches. There were even separate drinking fountains in the parks. During the 1960s, Dr. Martin Luther King, Jr. led African Americans and others who believed in justice in non-violent demonstrations. They were determined to win equal treatment. The Civil Rights Act of 1964 was followed by new laws protecting every citizen's access to jobs, voter registration and housing. Equal justice will not be won until all Americans empty their hearts of prejudice and hatred.

A PSALM FOR JULY

turn to
page 49

READING

Luke 6: 36–38

Listen to the words of the holy gospel according to Luke.

Jesus said to his disciples: "Don't judge others, and God won't judge you. Don't be hard on others, and God won't be hard on you. Forgive others, and God will forgive you. If you give to others, you will be given a full amount in return. It will be packed down, shaken together, and spilling over into you lap. the way you treat others is the way you will be treated."

The gospel of the Lord.

REFLECTION

How does my family help to make this a nation of justice and compassion? How have I helped to make this neighborhood a place of justice and compassion? Do I treat others as I want to be treated?

CLOSING

Let us remember these intentions:

God of all nations and creator of all peoples,
  heal all that divides your children
Teach us to live together in peace.
As our world is one, so our future is one.
Give us one heart and one vision.
Make us one body in Christ Jesus,
  filled with the joy of your Holy Spirit.
We ask this through Christ our Lord. **Amen.**

Let us pray with the words that Jesus taught us:

Our Father . . .

> sing
> "alleluia"

On this day in 1937 a brave pilot, Amelia Earhart, disappeared over the Pacific Ocean. She was trying to fly around the world. In your prayers today remember all who fly, and all who work to keep planes safe.

■ INTRODUCTION

Today we remember the apostle called Thomas, "the Twin." He is also called "Brave Thomas." When Jesus planned to go to Jerusalem even though it was dangerous, Thomas immediately said to the other apostles, "Come on. Let's go, so we can die with him." (John 11:16)

He is also called "Doubting Thomas." After today's reading, you will know why.

It is said that Thomas brought the good news to India, where many people came to believe in Jesus. There is a very old community there who call themselves "Christians of Saint Thomas."

■ A PSALM FOR JULY

➤ turn to
page 49

■ READING

John 20:24–28

Listen to the words of the holy gospel according to John.

Although Thomas the Twin was one of the twelve disciples, he wasn't with the others when Jesus appeared to them. So they told him, "We have seen the Lord!"

But Thomas said, "First, I must see the nail scars in his hands and touch them with my finger. I must put my hand where the spear went into his side. I won't believe unless I do this!"

A week later the disciples were together again. This time, Thomas was with them. Jesus came in while the doors were still locked and stood in the middle of the group. He greeted his disciples and said to Thomas, "Put your finger here and look at my hands. Put your hand into my side. Stop doubting and have faith!" Thomas replied, "You are my Lord and my God!"

The gospel of the Lord.

■ REFLECTION

What does it mean to address Jesus as "my Lord and my God"? How do members of my parish show that we believe in the resurrection of Jesus? How can I continue to strengthen my faith in Jesus?

■ CLOSING

Let us remember these intentions:

Jesus our brother,
   through the gift of your Spirit,
   and the teaching of the apostles,
   we proclaim that you are the risen savior:
   our Lord and our God.
Strengthen our faith,
   that we may praise you,
   now and for ever. **Amen.**

Let us pray with the words that Jesus taught us:

Our Father . . .

 sing
"alleluia"

Get ready for tomorrow! Put out the flag. Read the Declaration of Independence. Make a streamer or an apple pie.

JULY 4

INTRODUCTION

This is Independence Day, but you knew that!

On this day in the year 1776, the Declaration of Independence announced that 13 American colonies joined together to form a new nation. We are happy to be part of a country that declares the right of each person to "life, liberty and the pursuit of happiness." We honor its history and its heroes. We do what we can to protect the beauty of the land we have inherited.

A PSALM FOR JULY

▶ turn to
  page 49

READING

Psalm 146:3–9

Listen to the words of the book of Psalms.

Do not put your trust in rulers,
in mortals, in whom there is no help.
Their breath departs, they return to the earth;
on that very day their plans perish.

Happy are those whose help is in the God of
    Jacob,
whose hope is in the Lord, their God,
who made heaven and earth,
the sea, and all that is in them.

The Lord keeps faith forever,
executes justice for the oppressed,
gives food to the hungry.

The Lord sets the prisoners free;
the Lord opens the eyes of the blind.

The Lord lifts up those who are bowed down.
The Lord watches over the aliens,
and upholds the widow and the orphan.

The word of the Lord.

■ REFLECTION

Why is religious freedom so important? Why should people who were once oppressed be careful never to oppress others?

■ CLOSING

Let us remember these intentions:

People who are hungry are not free.
People who are afraid are not free.
People who are laughed at are not free.
Loving God,
    grant that next year we may celebrate
    in a land where everyone is free.
We ask this through Christ our Lord. **Amen.**

Let us pray with the words that Jesus taught us:

Our Father . . .

 sing
"alleluia"

Three presidents died on the 4th of July: Thomas Jefferson and John Adams in 1826, and James Monroe in 1831.

JULY 5

■ INTRODUCTION

When people of the church lead careless lives, and even leaders become corrupt or lazy, God seems to raise up holy people who show others how to reform their lives. Saint Anthony Zaccaria *(zuh-KAH-ree-uh)* was a person like that. He was born in Italy during the early 16th century, a sad time of warfare among Christians.

Anthony first became a doctor, then a priest. Then he formed societies of men and women who wanted to live holy lives. Anthony showed them how to care for the sick, teach the good news, and help others find the way back to Christ. It is said that he and the societies that he formed brought about a revival of the Christian spirit in the city of Milan.

■ A PSALM FOR JULY

turn to page 49

■ READING

Luke 10:1–9

Listen to the words of the holy gospel according to Luke.

The Lord chose seventy-two other followers and sent them out two by two to every town and village where he was about to go.

He said to them: "A large crop is in the fields, but there are only a few workers. Ask the Lord in charge of the harvest to send out workers to bring it in.

"Now go, but remember, I am sending you like lambs into a pack of wolves. Don't take along a moneybag or a traveling bag or sandals.

And don't waste time greeting people on the road. As soon as you enter a home, say, 'God bless this home with peace.' If the people living there are peace-loving, your prayer for peace will bless them. But if they are not peace-loving, your prayer will return to you."

The gospel of the Lord.

■ REFLECTION

What harvest is Jesus talking about? Who does Jesus send out today? Am I peace-loving?

■ CLOSING

Let us remember these intentions:

God of enduring love,
    source of our life
    and strength of our family,
    grant that our home may always be
    a place of welcome and peace.
We ask this through Christ our Lord. **Amen.**

Let us pray with the words that Jesus taught us

Our Father . . .

sing "alleluia"

Try to be a peacemaker today.

JULY 6

■ INTRODUCTION

Today we remember Saint Maria Goretti, who died when she was only 11. Maria's family worked on a farm in Italy. A neighbor boy began to sexually abuse Maria and when she resisted, he stabbed her. As she was dying, Maria forgave the boy, and prayed for him.

Even today, girls are sometimes treated with disrespect, as if their bodies were not the temples of the Holy Spirit that they are. All young people can pray for the wisdom, safety and courage they need as they grow up.

A PSALM FOR JULY

turn to page 49

■ READING

I Corinthians 6: 12, 13–15, 19–20

Listen to the words of the apostle Paul.

Some of you say, "We can do anything we want to." But I tell you that not everything is good for us. So I refuse to let anything have power over me. We are not supposed to do indecent things with our bodies. We are to use them for the Lord who is in charge of our bodies. God will raise us from death by the same power that he used when he raised our Lord to life.

Don't you know that your bodies are part of the body of Christ? You surely know that your body is a temple where the Holy Spirit lives. The Spirit is in you and is a gift from God. You are no longer your own. God paid a great price for you. So use your body to honor God.

The word of the Lord.

■ REFLECTION

Do I respect my body and treat it with care? Do I respect others' bodies as well? Do I turn away from TV shows or magazines that are not appropriate? Is there an adult I trust, an adult I can talk to if I am disturbed about something?

■ CLOSING

Psalm 139:13–16

Let us remember these intentions:

O Lord, you formed my inward parts,
you knit me together in my mother's womb.
I praise you, for I am fearfully
    and wonderfully made.
Wonderful are your works!
My frame was not hidden from you,
when I was being made in secret.
In your book were written
the days that were formed for me,
each day, before any existed.
Wonderful are your works!

Let us pray with the words that Jesus taught us:

Our Father . . .

 sing "alleluia"

On this day in 1866, Beatrix Potter was born. She wrote the tales of Peter Rabbit and put her own paintings in the book. She wrote other fine animal stories. Reread some of them today.

■ INTRODUCTION

People sometimes take the earth for granted. We are so used to finding it under our feet that we forget how fragile and complex it is.

One way to teach our eyes to look more closely is to take paper and paints or pencils outside and spend some time drawing what we see. You cannot draw a picture of a tree or flower, an ant or seashell, without looking closely at it. What are its colors? its shapes? its weight?

There are many ways to honor the planet and its Creator. Have a picnic, plant some seeds, read a science book from the library, climb a tree, count the vegetables in the grocery store, peel an orange and smell the oil on your hands.

■ A PSALM FOR JULY

 turn to page 49

■ READING

Genesis 2:4–9, 15

Listen to the words of the book of Genesis.

When the LORD God made the heavens and the earth, no grass or plants were growing anywhere. God had not yet sent any rain, and there was no one to work the land. But streams came up from the ground and watered the earth.

The LORD God took a handful of soil and made a man. God breathed life into the man, and the man started breathing. The LORD made a garden in a place called Eden, which was in the east, and he put the man there. The LORD placed all kinds of beautiful trees and fruit trees in the garden.

The LORD God put the man in the Garden of Eden to take care of it and to look after it.

The word of the Lord.

■ REFLECTION

What am I doing this summer to care for the earth? Have I begun a garden that needs tending? Do I care for my pets or other creatures that share the earth with me? Do I notice the beauty of the world around me?

■ CLOSING

Let us remember these intentions:

Blessed are you, Lord our God,
    creator of the universe.
You give the world to us as a home,
    and fill it with your glory.
Teach us to recognize its wonders,
    to treasure its variety,
    and to protect its fragile beauty.
We ask this through Christ our Lord. **Amen.**

Let us pray with the words that Jesus taught us.

Our Father . . .

 sing "alleluia"

Today Japanese children celebrate Tanabata, a star festival. They write poems on bright paper and tie them with threads to porches and bamboo poles. This is a good night to make some wishes on stars.

JULY 8

■ INTRODUCTION

Today we remember a married couple, Saints Priscilla and Aquila (*priss-ILL-uh* and *ACK-will-uh*). They were leaders in the church in Corinth, and Saint Paul stayed with them when he came to town. The three worked together, making tents and preaching the word of God. After a while they moved to Rome. Paul wrote to the Christians there, "Give my greetings to Priscilla and Aquila. They have not only served Christ Jesus together with me, but they have even risked their lives for me. Greet the church that meets in their home."

■ A PSALM FOR JULY

turn to
page 49

■ READING

Acts 2:42–47

Listen to the words of the Acts of the Apostles.

[Those who were baptized] spent their time learning from the apostles, and they were like family to each other. They also broke bread and prayed together.

Everyone was amazed by the many miracles and wonders that the apostles worked. All the Lord's followers often met together, and they shared everything they had. They would sell their property and possessions and give the money to whoever needed it. Day after day they met together in the temple. They broke bread together in different homes and shared their food happily and freely, while praising God. Everyone liked them, and each day the Lord added to their group others who were being saved.

The word of the Lord.

■ REFLECTION

How is my parish "like family to each other"? How do they share what they have? How are new people added to our Christian family?

■ CLOSING

Let us remember these intentions:

Faithful God,
Fill us with your grace,
   so that our words and our works
   may proclaim the coming of your kingdom.
We ask this through Christ our Lord. **Amen.**

Let us pray with the words that Jesus taught us:

Our Father . . .

sing
"alleluia"

On this day in 1835, the Liberty Bell cracked when it was rung for the funeral of John Marshall, Chief Justice of the Supreme Court. Today fix something that is broken.

■ INTRODUCTION

Today we remember Augustus Tolton, the son of slaves, who could not find an American Catholic seminary willing to accept an African American student. He studied in Rome and was ordained there. When Augustus returned, he became the pastor of an African American parish, where his spirited preaching and leadership soon attracted white members. This upset many people. Even his bishop thought that Augustus "wants to establish a kind of society here that is not possible," meaning integration. Father Tolton died in 1897, almost 50 years before Catholics of all races learned to worship together.

■ A PSALM FOR JULY

turn to page 49

■ READING

Matthew 5:1–4, 7–10

Listen to the words of the holy gospel according to Matthew.

Jesus' disciples gathered around him, and he taught them:
"God blesses those people
    who depend only on God.
    They belong to the kingdom of heaven!
God blesses those people who grieve (greev).
    They will find comfort!
God blesses those people who are merciful.
    They will be treated with mercy!
God blesses those people whose hearts are pure.
    They will see God!

God blesses those people who make peace.
    They will be called God's children!
God blesses those people
    who are treated badly for doing right.
They belong to the kingdom of heaven."

The gospel of the Lord.

■ REFLECTION

God's blessings in the gospel are called "the beatitudes." What additional beatitudes might Jesus compose for families today? How do people in my family live the beatitudes?

■ CLOSING

Let us remember these intentions:

O God, wherever you find evil,
    you send a promise of salvation.
May our choices always lead to good.
And may we help to end the evil
    that we see around us.
We ask this through Christ our Lord. **Amen.**

Let us pray with the words that Jesus taught us

Our Father . . .

sing "alleluia"

On this day in 1868, the 14th amendment to the Constitution was ratified. It guarantees all citizens "due process" and equal protection under the law. Find out what this means to your family.

58

INTRODUCTION

Celebrate water today! It covers 71 percent of our planet and makes the sky seem blue. It enables us to farm, fish, wash and swim. The earliest forms of life appeared in the oceans, and we are reborn in the waters of baptism.

But this gift of God is endangered by chemicals pouring from farms and factories. Isn't it amazing that we are careless of a resource on which our lives depend!

A PSALM FOR JULY

▶ turn to
page 49

READING

John 4:8–11, 13–14

Listen to the words of the holy gospel according to John.

A Samaritan woman came to draw water from the well. Jesus asked her, "Would you please give me a drink of water?"

"You are a Jew," she replied, "and I am a Samaritan woman. How can you ask me for a drink of water when Jews and Samaritans won't have anything to do with each other?" Jesus answered, "You don't know what God wants to give you, and you don't know who is asking you for a drink. If you did, you would ask me for the water that gives life."

"Sir," the woman said, "you don't even have a bucket, and the well is deep. Where are you going to get this life-giving water?" Jesus answered, "Everyone who drinks this water will get thirsty again. But no one who drinks the water I give will ever be thirsty again."

The gospel of the Lord.

REFLECTION

Why is water a good symbol for all of God's gifts to us? How does my family try to save water?

CLOSING

Let us remember these intentions:

God our Creator, source of living water,
  you make the desert bloom,
  and dry lands bear fruit.
In the waters of baptism we are reborn
  through the power of your Spirit,
  and the grace of Christ Jesus.
For the gift of water we praise you,
  for ever and ever. **Amen.**

Let us pray with the words that Jesus taught us:

Our Father . . .

▶ sing
"alleluia"

On this day in 1882, Governor Hogg of Texas named his newborn daughter Ima. All her life, Ima was embarrassed by cruel jokes, though she was a kind person. Make a promise never to make fun of anyone's name.

JULY 11

■ INTRODUCTION

Today we remember Saint Benedict, the patron of Europe. Early in the sixth century, Benedict went into the hills near his home to lead a life of prayer. Others came to join him so he organized their days together. He wrote a guide called the Holy Rule, which set aside times each day for prayer, study, work and rest. The Holy Rule makes for a very balanced way of life.

Today thousands of Benedictine monks and nuns around the world follow Benedict's Holy Rule. They are known for their generosity in taking in strangers and treating them as they would treat Christ.

■ A PSALM FOR JULY

turn to
page 49

■ READING

Proverbs 2:4–9

Listen to the words of the book of Proverbs.

Search for wisdom as you would search for silver or hidden treasure. Then you will understand what it means to respect and to know the LORD God.

All wisdom comes from the LORD, and so do common sense and understanding. God gives helpful advice to everyone who obeys him and protects all of those who live as they should. God sees that justice is done, and watches over everyone who is faithful to him. With wisdom you will learn what is right and honest and fair.

The word of the Lord.

■ REFLECTION

Do I take time for prayer every day? Do I balance play and chores? Is my diet balanced? there some part of my life that needs to be balanced with the rest?

■ CLOSING

Let us remember these intentions:

All you creatures of the Lord, bless the Lord.
   Praise and glorify God for ever.
Light and darkness, praise the Lord.
Heat and coldness, praise the Lord.
Grown-ups and children, praise the Lord.
   Praise and glorify God for ever.
Fullbacks and ballerinas, praise the Lord.
Giraffes and caterpillars, praise the Lord.
Ice cream and green peas, praise the Lord.
   Praise and glorify God for ever.
We offer God all praise
   through Christ our Lord. **Amen.**

Let us pray with the words that Jesus taught us

Our Father . . .

sing
"alleluia"

Experiment with balance today: roller skate, juggle, bu a house of cards. Grown-ups can try to balance the checkbooks.

JULY 12

■ INTRODUCTION

Today we remember Veronica, whose name means "true image." According to an ancient legend, she saw Jesus' suffering as he was carrying the cross. Out of kindness, she wiped his face with her veil, and found that his image remained on the fabric. Veronica's legend was very popular in the Middle Ages, and it was added to the Stations of the Cross. (Look at Station Six in your church.)

We do not know whether Veronica really existed. But she is a "true image" of everyone who sees Christ suffering in other people, and offers kindness.

■ A PSALM FOR JULY

 turn to
page 49

■ READING
Matthew 10:40–42

Listen to the words of the holy gospel according to Matthew.

Jesus said to his disciples: "Anyone who welcomes you welcomes me. And anyone who welcomes me also welcomes the one who sent me.

"Anyone who welcomes a prophet, just because that person is a prophet, will be given the same reward as a prophet. Anyone who welcomes a good person, just because that person is good, will be given the same reward as a good person.

"And anyone who gives one of my most humble followers a cup of cool water, just because that person is my follower, will surely be rewarded."

The gospel of the Lord.

■ REFLECTION

What kindness have members of my family shown to others? Why is it easier to be kind when we remember that Christ lives within the other person? Who has shown kindness to me?

■ CLOSING

Let us remember these intentions:

Loving God,
   make us attentive to the sufferings
   of your Son in other people.
And make our hearts generous
   in showing kindness to all.
We ask this through Christ our Lord. **Amen.**

Let us pray with the words that Jesus taught us:

Our Father . . .

 sing
"alleluia"

An early ecologist, Henry David Thoreau, was born on this day in 1817. He wrote, "I frequently tramped eight or ten miles through the deepest snow to keep an appointment with a beech tree, or a yellow birch, or an old acquaintance among the pines." There won't be any snow to keep us from visiting some tree friends today!

■ INTRODUCTION

We all want to be important. We want to be noticed, invited to big parties, and given gifts. Sometimes we feel important if a famous person writes to us, so we show that letter to our friends. Sometimes being on a winning team or having our picture in the paper gives us the feeling that we are somebody special.

One day Jesus was invited to dinner by an important person, and he saw the other guests showing off. He pointed out to them that people who take the best seats can be embarrassed when someone more important arrives and they have to move. It is better not to puff yourself up. Then others who know your real worth can honor you.

■ A PSALM FOR JULY

 turn to
page 49

■ READING

Luke 14:1, 12–14

Listen to the words of the holy gospel according to Luke.

One Sabbath Jesus was having dinner in the home of an important Pharisee, and everyone was carefully watching Jesus.

Jesus said to the man who had invited him: "When you give a dinner or a banquet, don't invite your friends and family and relatives and rich neighbors. If you do, they will invite you in return, and you will be paid back.

When you give a feast, invite the poor, the crippled, the lame, and the blind. They cannot pay you back. But God will bless you and reward you."

The gospel of the Lord.

■ REFLECTION

What do I do without expecting to be paid back? How does my family share its feast with the poor? How can I share the feast of friendship with people who are not in my circle of friends? How will people behave at the banquet in God's kingdom?

■ CLOSING

Let us remember these intentions:

Loving God,
  make us attentive to the sufferings
  of your Son in other people.
And make our hearts generous
  in showing kindness to all.
We ask this through Christ our Lord. **Amen.**

Let us pray with the words that Jesus taught us

Our Father . . .

 sing
"alleluia"

Make a new friend today. Show an old friend a kindness

JULY 14

■ INTRODUCTION

Today we remember Blessed Kateri Tekakwitha (CAT-uh-ree teh-KOK-with-uh), "The Lily of the Mohawks." Her father was a Mohawk chief and her mother a Christian Algonquin. When she was four, they died of smallpox, and Kateri was left scarred and almost blind. (Tekakwitha means "one who feels her way along.")

When Kateri was eleven, missionaries came to her village. She was baptized on Easter Sunday, 1676, and soon moved to a Christian village. She tended the sick, cared for children and spent many hours in prayer. She died in 1680 at the age of 24.

■ A PSALM FOR JULY

turn to
page 49

■ READING

John 6:63–64, 66–69

Listen to the words of the holy gospel according to John.

Jesus said to his disciples, "The Spirit is the one who gives life! Human strength can do nothing. The words that I have spoken to you are from that life-giving Spirit. But some of you refuse to have faith in me."

Because of what Jesus said, many of his disciples turned their backs on him and stopped following him. Jesus then asked his twelve disciples if they were going to leave him. Simon Peter answered, "Lord, there is no one else that we can go to! Your words give eternal life. We have faith in you, and we are sure that you are God's Holy One."

The gospel of the Lord.

■ REFLECTION

Have I stopped following Jesus during the summer? Am I so sure of my faith that I fail to study the words of Jesus? How can I be as faithful to Jesus in my life as Kateri Tekakwitha was?

■ CLOSING

Let us remember these intentions:

Lord God,
    you led Kateri Tekakwitha
    to give you her whole life and energy.
Share your life and your Spirit
    with all your people.
Make us faithful and true.
We ask this through Christ our Lord. **Amen.**

Let us pray with the words that Jesus taught us:

Our Father . . .

sing
"alleluia"

Happy Bastille Day! On July 14, 1798, the French people overthrew the king and freed the prisoners from the dungeons of the Bastille. The key to the hated prison was given to George Washington, because he had shown the world how to govern a free republic. Guess what colors the French people put into their new flag!

■ INTRODUCTION

Today we remember Saint Bonaventure, often called the "second founder" of the Franciscans. He was one of the best students at the University of Paris when great theologians were studying there. His friend Thomas Aquinas was also there, and they both were writing great works of theology.

Soon the Franciscans called on Bonaventure to become their leader, and he was good at that too. It was only twelve years after Saint Francis had died, and his followers did not know how best to carry on his work. Bonaventure listened to everyone, made good decisions and did not put on airs. He died in 1274, and was named a "Doctor of the Church," which means a great teacher.

■ A PSALM FOR JULY

turn to page 49

■ READING

Ephesians 4:11–13, 15–16

Listen to the words of the apostle Paul.

Christ chose some of us to be apostles, prophets, missionaries, pastors, and teachers, so that his people would learn to serve and his body would grow strong. This will continue until we are united by our faith and by our understanding of the son of god. Then we will be mature, just as Christ is, and we will be completely like him.

Love should always make us tell the truth. Then we will grow in every way and be more like Christ, the head of the body. Christ holds it together and makes all of its parts work perfect as it grows and becomes strong because of lov

The word of the Lord.

■ REFLECTION

How does good leadership strengthen the mer bers of a community? Am I growing "stror because of love" this summer?

■ CLOSING

Let us remember these intentions:

Loving God,
    bless the leaders of our family
    and our community.
Draw all of us closer to you
    and to one another this summer.
We ask this through Christ our Lord. **Amen.**

Let us pray with the words that Jesus taught u

Our Father . . .

sing "alleluia"

In England this is Saint Swithun's Day named for a we loved bishop who died in 862. Look outside and pred the weather for the next weeks with this poem.

St. Swithun's Day, if thou dost rain,
for 40 days it will remain.

St. Swithun's Day, if thou be fair,
for 40 days 'twill rain nae mair (that means "no more"

JULY 16

INTRODUCTION

Today is the feast of Our Lady of Mount Carmel, a day of celebration for Carmelite men and women around the world.

Mount Carmel is in Israel. It is a sacred place where God's power was revealed through the work of the prophet Elijah. From the first century, Christian hermits lived there. By the year 1200, a religious community had been formed. They were devoted to Mary and called her Our Lady of Mount Carmel. They soon spread around the world, doing public ministries or living in solitude. Carmelite communities have given many famous mystics to the church.

A PSALM FOR JULY

▶ turn to
page 49

READING

Luke 1:46–51, 53–55

Listen to the words of the holy gospel according to Luke.

Mary said:
With all my heart I praise the Lord,
    and I am glad because of God my Savior.
God cares for me, his humble servant.
From now on, all people will say
    God has blessed me.
God All-Powerful has done great things for me,
    and his name is holy.
He always shows mercy to everyone who
    worships him.
The Lord has used his powerful arm
    to scatter those who are proud.

God gives the hungry good things to eat,
    and sends the rich away with nothing.
God helps his servant Israel,
    and is always merciful to his people."

The gospel of the Lord.

■ REFLECTION

Why do people give Mary many titles? The Carmelites are prayerful like Mary. How am I like her? What can I learn from studying her "magnificat" (today's reading)?

■ CLOSING

Let us remember these intentions:

Loving God, you give us your finest grace,
    your greatest blessing.
You give us yourself.
In Christ, you share our life.
In Christ, you share our suffering and our joy.
All glory to you, now and for ever. **Amen.**

Let us pray with the words that Jesus taught us:

Our Father . . .

 sing
"alleluia"

On this day in 1867, D.R. Averill of Ohio was granted a patent for ready-mixed paint. Celebrate by painting something wonderful—a picture, a chair, your toenails!

■ INTRODUCTION

Yesterday we learned about the Carmelite order. Today we remember 16 Carmelite sisters of Compiègne *(kohm-PYEN)*, France, who gave their lives for the right to worship God freely.

During the French revolution, some horrible things happened. The revolutionary government outlawed religious orders, and the sisters of Compiègne had to leave their convent, put away their religious clothing, and pray only in secret. Even so, 16 of them were arrested. In prison they bravely took up their religious clothing again, and their prayer. On July 17, 1794, they were taken to their execution singing the psalms and the prayers for the dying. Like Christian martyrs in every century, they were willing to die with Christ, knowing that they would rise with him to glory.

■ A PSALM FOR JULY

turn to page 49

■ READING
Romans 8:35, 37–39

Listen to the words of the apostle Paul.

Brothers and sisters: Can anything separate us from the love of Christ? Can trouble, suffering, and hard times, or hunger and nakedness, or danger and death?

In everything we have won more than a victory because of Christ who loves us.

I am sure that nothing can separate us from God's love—not life or death, not angels or spirits, not the present or the future, and not powers above or powers below. Nothing in all creation can separate us from God's love for us in Chri[st] Jesus our Lord!

The word of the Lord.

■ REFLECTION

Does anything try to separate me from the lo[ve] of Christ? Have I been as close to God this sum[mer] as I want to be? Is there some difficulty th[at] I am facing because of my love for God?

■ CLOSING

Let us remember these intentions:

Loving God,
   you call us your children
   and save us through your own suffering.
Defend us against evil.
Make us brave and faithful,
   and strengthen us in times of trouble.
We ask this through Christ our Lord. **Amen.**

Let us pray with the words that Jesus taught u[s]

Our Father . . .

sing
"alleluia"

On this day in 1938, Douglas Corrigan took off from [an] airfield in New York to fly non-stop to California. H[e] landed 28 hours and 13 minutes later—in Dubl[in,] Ireland! He has been called "Wrong-way Corrigan" ev[er] since, for following the wrong end of his compass need[le.] This is a day to check your compass and be sure you a[re] flying in the right direction.

INTRODUCTION

day we remember Bartolome de Las Casas
r-tow-low-MAY day lahs KAH-sahs), a
anish priest who came to Cuba with the con-
istadores *(kon-KEES-tuh-doors)* to teach the
tive peoples about Christ. He soon saw that
e conquistadores' hearts were set on gold
ther than the gospel. They were murdering
d enslaving native peoples. De Las Casas tried
end the abuses, but he was laughed at.
To get rid of him, officials sent de Las Casas to
e southern tip of Mexico, as bishop of Chiapas
ee-AH-pas). He worked hard for his people
til he died in 1566. Even today the natives of
iapas are struggling for just treatment.

A PSALM FOR JULY

 turn to
page 49

READING

Jeremiah 23: 3–5

ten to the words of the prophet Jeremiah.
he LORD, will bring the rest of my people
   back from the lands where
   I have scattered them.
ill bring them home,
   and they will grow into a mighty nation.
ill choose leaders who will take care of them.
ery one of my people will be there,
   and they will never again be frightened
   or terrified.
he LORD, have spoken.
romise that the time will come
   when I will choose a king from the family
   of David.

He will be wise and will rule the land
   with justice and fairness.

The word of the Lord.

■ REFLECTION

Do I defend people I see mistreated? If my family or nation were being unjust, would I speak
up? Do my friends treat everyone justly?

■ CLOSING

Let us remember these intentions:

O God,
   wherever you find evil,
   you send a promise of salvation.
May our choices always lead to good.
And may we help to end the evil
   that we see around us.
We ask this through Christ our Lord. **Amen.**

Let us pray with the words that Jesus taught us:

Our Father . . .

 sing
"alleluia"

Explore Hispanic culture: eat Mexican food, play Hispanic
music and games, find Spanish words we use every day,
list sports figures, find out about festivals important to
people from Central and South America.

■ INTRODUCTION

Today we remember Saint Macrina *(mah-CREE-nuh),* who came from a very surprising family. Macrina, her parents and three brothers are listed among the church's saints.

Macrina helped her ten younger brothers and sisters with their studies. She taught them about the Bible as well. With that start, her brothers Gregory and Basil became important theologians. She died in the year 379.

We can learn something from Macrina's family. They played, prayed and worked together. They encouraged each other to live a Christian life. They were a household church.

■ A PSALM FOR JULY

 turn to page 49

■ READING

Exodus 19:1–6

Listen to the words of the book of Exodus.

Two months after the people of Israel left Egypt, they reached the desert near Mount Sinai. They set up camp there at the foot of the mountain.

Moses went up the mountain to meet with the LORD God, who told him to say to the people:

"You saw what I, the LORD, did in Egypt. You know how like a mighty eagle I brought you here to me. Now if you will obey me and are faithful to me, you will be my people. The whole world is mine. But you will be mine in a special way and serve me as priests."

The word of the Lord.

■ REFLECTION

Do the members of my family treat each other the Lord's own people—as members of a house hold church? How can I encourage my broth and sisters to grow in their love of God?

■ CLOSING

Let us remember these intentions:

We thank you, O God,
  for keeping us in safety,
  and making us your people.
Strengthen our family in our love for you.
And help us to bring your love
  to the world we share.
We ask this through Christ our Lord. **Amen.**

Let us pray with the words that Jesus taught u

Our Father . . .

 sing "alleluia"

On this day in 1834, Edgar Degas *(deh-GAH)* was born Paris, France. He became an artist, and did many famc drawings of ballet dancers. Do some dancing today honor of Degas.

JULY 20

INTRODUCTION

■day we remember Leo XIII, who was pope ▪r 25 years, and died in 1903, just as the twen-▪th century began. He did many things to open ▪e eyes of the church to events going on in the ▪orld. He invited scholars into the Vatican ▪raries. He encouraged Catholics to study the ▪ble. And he urged all in the church to take an ▪terest in people's social and material needs, not ▪st their spiritual welfare.

▪ Leo XIII outlined principles of social justice, ▪e dignity of labor, and the defense of the poor. ▪e challenged God's people: "Some remedy ▪ust be found, and quickly found, for the mis-▪y and wretchedness which press so heavily at ▪is moment on the large majority of the very ▪or." As the twenty-first century begins, this ▪sk remains unfinished.

A PSALM FOR JULY

 turn to
page 49

READING

Isaiah 58: 6–8

▪sten to the words of the prophet Isaiah.

▪ tell you what it really means to worship the ▪RD. Remove the chains of prisoners who are ▪ained unjustly. Free those who are abused! ▪are your food with everyone who is hungry; ▪are your home with the poor and homeless. ▪ve clothes to those in need; don't turn away ▪ur relatives. Then your light will shine like the ▪wning sun, and you will quickly be healed.

▪e word of the Lord.

■ REFLECTION

It is not too late to make plans to share time this summer with someone who needs us. Who needs a smile? a hug? toys or clothes we don't use any more? What would Isaiah want people our age to do?

■ CLOSING

Let us remember these intentions:

Loving God,
    we thank you for giving our family
    your gifts of food and love.
We have been cared for and protected.
We have eaten and been filled.
Show us how to share what we have been given,
    and to be your worthy disciples.
We ask this through Christ our Lord. **Amen.**

Let us pray with the words that Jesus taught us:

Our Father . . .

 sing
"alleluia"

On this day in 1969, the first human footprints were placed on the moon. Can you name the two astronauts who made that journey? (Their last names begin with "A.") They discovered that the moon is not made of green cheese after all.

■ INTRODUCTION

Today we remember Albert Luthuli, who died on this day in 1967. He was a Zulu chief in South Africa during the time of apartheid *(uh-PART-hite)*. This was a system of laws depriving black citizens of their right to live, work, marry or travel as they chose. People who wanted to end this injustice formed the African National Congress, with Albert as its leader. He organized strikes and other forms of non-violent resistance. He was beaten and arrested many times, but he wrote, "In working for freedom some individuals and some families must take the lead and suffer: The road to freedom is the Cross."

In 1960 Albert Luthuli was awarded the Nobel Peace Prize. After years of suffering, change has finally come to South Africa.

■ A PSALM FOR JULY

turn to
page 49

■ READING

Matthew 11:28–30

Listen to the words of the holy gospel according to Matthew.

Jesus said, "If you are tired from carrying heavy burdens, come to me and I will give you rest. Take the yoke I give you. Put it on your shoulders and learn from me. I am gentle and humble, and you will find rest. This yoke is easy to bear, and this burden is light."

The gospel of the Lord.

70

■ REFLECTION

How can we help those who are struggling f justice? Do I use only non-violent ways to ga justice for myself? What are some non-viole ways to deal with injustice in my neighborhoo

■ CLOSING

Let us remember these intentions:

O God,
  wherever you find evil,
  you send a promise of salvation.
May our choices always lead to good.
And may we help to end the evil
  that we see around us.
We ask this through Christ our Lord. **Amen.**

Let us pray with the words that Jesus taught u

Our Father . . .

sing
"alleluia"

One of the people who was inspired by Albert Luth was a young lawyer. He spent 28 years in prison rath than give up the struggle for freedom. Later he becam the first black president of South Africa. His name Nelson Mandela.

INTRODUCTION

…day we remember Mary Magdalene, who …s very dear to Jesus. She went along on Jesus' …aching journeys. She followed him to Calvary, …d she stayed with him until he died. She was …o one of the women who went to the tomb … anoint his body. As we hear in today's read-…, Mary was the first to see the risen Lord. …Because Mary Magdalene brought the good …ws of Christ's resurrection to the Twelve, she …alled "apostle to the apostles."

A PSALM FOR JULY

turn to
page 49

READING

John 20:11–16

…ten to the words of the holy gospel according …John.

…ary Magdalene stood crying outside the tomb. …e was still weeping, when she stooped down …d saw two angels inside. They were dressed …white and were sitting where Jesus' body had …en. One was at the head and the other was …the foot. The angels asked Mary, "Why are …u crying?"

…She answered, "They have taken away my …rd's body! I don't know where they have put …n." As soon as Mary said this, she turned …und and saw Jesus standing there. But she did …t know who he was. Jesus asked her, "Why …e you crying? Who are you looking for?"

…She thought he was the gardener and said, "Sir, …ou have taken his body away, please tell me,

so I can go and get him." Then Jesus said to her, "Mary!" She turned and said to him, "Teacher."

The gospel of the Lord.

■ REFLECTION

How does Jesus make me aware of his presence? Am I a messenger of good news? Who are some holy women who have taught me about Jesus?

■ CLOSING

Let us remember these intentions:

Gracious God,
    through the joyful words of Mary Magdalene
    you bring the good news of your love
    to all the peoples of the earth.
Strengthen us to carry that good news
    in our lives, in our hearts and in our words.
We ask this through Christ our Lord. **Amen.**

Let us pray with the words that Jesus taught us:

Our Father . . .

sing
"alleluia"

Centuries ago people did not have last names, so they were often named for their home town. Mary came from the town of Magdala, so she was called Mary the Magdalene.

■ INTRODUCTION

Today we remember Saint Bridget, the patron of Sweden. Bridget had a happy marriage and raised eight children. She also took seriously the command of the gospel to care for those beyond her family. She provided for the poor, and had a hospital built where she tended the sick. After her husband died and her children were grown, Bridget gave her possessions away and went to a monastery to devote more time to prayer. From her childhood she had received insights and visions while praying.

Even at the monastery God gave her work to do. She wrote scolding letters to popes and rulers, urging them to be more just and honest. She traveled to the holy places of Europe and the Holy Land, and died in Rome in 1373.

■ A PSALM FOR JULY

turn to
page 49

■ READING

Luke 10:25–28

Listen to the words of the holy gospel according to Luke.

An expert in the Law of Moses stood up and asked Jesus a question. "Teacher," he asked, "What must I do to have eternal life?"

Jesus answered, "What is written in the Scriptures? How do you understand them?"

The man replied, "The Scriptures say, 'Love the Lord your God with all your heart, soul, strength, and mind.' They also say, 'Love your neighbors as much as you love yourself.'"

Jesus said, "You have given the right answer. If you do this, you will have eternal life."

The gospel of the Lord.

■ REFLECTION

How did Saint Bridget follow the two commandments that Jesus gave us? How do I follow each of them? This reading is the heart of Christ's message. Do we know it by heart?

■ CLOSING

Let us remember these intentions:

God of grace and wisdom,
  you give us your word
  to teach and guide us.
And you continually raise up good people
  who show with their lives
  that they follow a holy and loving God.
Let our lives be as true as our faith.
We ask this through Christ our Lord. **Amen.**

Let us pray with the words that Jesus taught us

Our Father . . .

sing
"alleluia"

On this day in 1904, Charles Menches sold the first cream cones at the Louisiana Purchase Exposition Saint Louis, Missouri. He was running out of dishes at ice cream stand, so he folded thin waffles into holde Enjoy a Menches masterpiece today!

JULY 24

INTRODUCTION

[To]day we remember Saint Thomas à Kempis [(ah KEM-*pis*),] who died in 1471. He belonged [to] a religious order in which priests and lay [m]embers read the Bible each day and tried to [pu]t its teachings into their lives.

[St.] Thomas wrote a book to help people reflect [on] God's action in their lives. It has been trans[la]ted into more languages than any other book [ex]cept the Bible. It is called *The Imitation of [Ch]rist,* and it influenced the spirituality of both [C]atholics and Protestants. Ask your grandpar[en]ts if they have ever read it.

A PSALM FOR JULY

turn to
page 49

READING

Deuteronomy 30:10–14

[Li]sten to the words of the book of Deuteronomy.

[M]oses said to the people: "You must obey the [LO]RD your God and follow all the laws and [co]mmands that are in the book of the Law. You [m]ust trust him with all your heart and soul. [T]hat I am commanding you today is not too [ha]rd. It isn't out of your reach somewhere up in [th]e sky. You don't have to ask yourselves, 'Who [w]ill go up to the sky and get it for us? Who will [br]ing it down and tell us what we must do?' [T]hat I am commanding you is not on the other [si]de of the sea. You don't have to ask yourselves, ['W]ho will cross the sea and get it for us? Who [w]ill bring it here and tell us what to do?' No!

What I am commanding is as near as your mouth or your heart. All you have to do is obey."

The word of the Lord.

REFLECTION

What does it mean that God's law is "as near as your mouth or your heart"? When I read the Bible do I ask myself what its meaning is for me? How can we imitate Christ? What religious books do people in my house read regularly?

CLOSING

Let us remember these intentions:

Loving and glorious God,
    we thank you for the gift of books
    and for the men and women
    who teach, guide and inspire us
    through the written word.
Draw near to us as we read of your wonders.
We ask this through Christ our Lord. **Amen.**

Let us pray with the words that Jesus taught us:

Our Father . . .

sing
"alleluia"

On this day in 1783, Simon Bolivar *(see-MOWN BOH-lee-vahr)* was born. He is called "The Liberator," and "George Washington of South America." Find on a map the country named for him.

73

■ INTRODUCTION

Today is the feast of Saint James the apostle. James and his brother John were working as fishermen when Jesus called them to be his disciples. They must have been energetic and excitable people, as Jesus nicknamed them the "sons of thunder." James was one of the three closest men to Jesus. He was present when Jesus raised the daughter of Jairus from the dead and in the Garden of Olives. And he may have been the first of the apostles to die for preaching about Jesus.

It is believed that James' bones were taken to Compostela in Spain. His shrine there was, after Rome and Jerusalem, the most popular place of pilgrimage during the Middle Ages.

■ A PSALM FOR JULY

turn to
page 49

■ READING

Matthew 20:20–23

Listen to the words of the holy gospel according to Matthew.

The mother of James and John came to Jesus with her two sons. She knelt down and started begging him to do something for her. Jesus asked her what she wanted, and she said, "When you come into your kingdom, please let one of my sons sit at your right side and the other at your left."

Jesus answered, "Not one of you knows what you are asking. Are you able to drink from the cup that I must soon drink from?" James and John said, "Yes, we are!"

Jesus replied, "You certainly will drink from my cup! But it isn't for me to say who will sit at my right side and at my left. That is for my Father to say."

The gospel of the Lord.

■ REFLECTION

Do I want the best place wherever I go? What cup did James and John drink from? What cup has Jesus offered to me?

■ CLOSING

Let us remember these intentions:

Lord God, we thank you
   for sending apostles to the whole world.
We welcome those who bring your good news.
We pray for them
   and listen to their teaching.
Call on us, one day, to become apostles, too.
We ask this through Christ our Lord. **Amen.**

Let us pray with the words that Jesus taught us.

Our Father . . .

sing
"alleluia"

Pilgrims to the shrine of Santiago ("Santiago" means "Saint James" in Spanish) de Compostela wore a scallop shell on their clothes, and people of the villages they passed through showed them hospitality. Have you ever brought home shells as a reminder of your travels?

INTRODUCTION

day we celebrate the couple who were Mary's
rents—and Jesus' grandparents! They are
own to us as Joachim and Ann, even though
eir names are not given in the Bible. Legends
l us that they waited for a child many years
fore Mary was born, and that they took her
the Temple at the age of three and dedicated
r to God. This is a day to do something loving
r grandparents in honor of Joachim and Ann.
Ann is the patron of Canada. A chapel dedi-
ted to her was built in 1658 in the town of
aupré *(bow-PRAY)*, Canada. A great church
there now, and thousands of pilgrims go there
this feast for the liturgy, a candlelight proces-
on and a blessing of the sick.

■ REFLECTION

I have seen and heard Jesus in ways that many
people in this world have not. Why has God
blessed me? What has God shown me that is
true? Who has loved and protected us the way
Joachim and Ann cared for Mary?

■ CLOSING

Let us remember these intentions:

A PSALM FOR JULY

 turn to
page 49

READING

Matthew 13: 16–17

sten to the words of the holy gospel according
Matthew.

sus said, "God has blessed you, because your
es can see and your ears can hear! Many
ophets and good people were eager to see
hat you see and to hear what you hear. But I
l you that they did not see or hear."

he gospel of the Lord.

God of unchanging love,
    as you prepared a family to receive Jesus,
        your Son,
    and blessed their home with his presence,
    so help my family to welcome Christ.
Let him be our guide and protector,
    until we are gathered into our heavenly home.
We ask this through Christ our Lord. **Amen.**

Let us pray with the words that Jesus taught us:

Our Father . . .

 sing
"alleluia"

Ann's name is similar to that of Hannah, the mother of
Samuel. She also waited many years for a child, and then
dedicated him to God at the age of three. You can read
that story in I Samuel, chapters I to 3.

■ INTRODUCTION

Today we remember a German woman of the thirteenth century named Mechthild *(MEK-tild)*. From the age of twelve, Mechthild had strong experiences of God's presence. She believed that all people were meant to have the sure knowledge about God that she had. A person's age or amount of education did not matter.

She spent her life praying and being of service to people in need. She kept a journal, which gives helpful advice about Christian life. She wrote: "I tell you in truth: When I hold back a smile which would harm no one, or have a sourness in my heart which I tell to no one, or feel some impatience with my own pain, then my soul becomes dark and my heart cold."

■ A PSALM FOR JULY

turn to
page 49

■ READING

I Kings 19:9, 11–13

Listen to the words of the first book of Kings.

Elijah reached Mount Sinai, the mountain of God, and he spent the night there in a cave. The LORD said, "Elijah, go out and stand on the mountain. I want you to see me when I pass by."

All at once, a strong wind shook the mountain and shattered the rocks. But the LORD was not in the wind. Next, there was an earthquake, but the LORD was not in the earthquake. Then there was a fire, but the LORD was not in the fire.

Finally, there was a gentle breeze, and when Elijah heard it, he covered his face with his coat. He went out and stood at the entrance the cave.

The word of the Lord.

■ REFLECTION

Mechthild heard God when she was only twelv Am I waiting to grow up before I really listen f God's voice? Elijah heard God in a gentle breez Am I waiting for a big flashy miracle before take God seriously? How do we make ourselv ready to hear God?

■ CLOSING

Let us remember these intentions:

Gracious God,
   through the presence of your Spirit
   you hear and answer us.
Strengthen in us the gift of prayer,
   and deepen in us the blessing of faith.
We ask this through Christ our Lord. **Amen.**

Let us pray with the words that Jesus taught u

Our Father . . .

sing
"alleluia"

The word "spirit" comes from the Latin word f "breath" or "breeze." Can you think of other stories the Bible where God's Spirit is present? What other sig of the Spirit's action are there? (Check out Genesis I Exodus 19:16, and Acts 2:2.) Fly a kite in the breez today in honor of the Holy Spirit.

◀ INTRODUCTION

Today we remember Stanley Rother *(ROW-er)*, a good shepherd who gave his life for his flock. He was sent by the church in Oklahoma to serve a poor parish in Guatemala *(gwah-tuh-MAH-luh)*. Father Rother traveled through the countryside to visit all the people. He helped find food and medicine. He organized weaving and food cooperatives.

But some people did not want the Indians to be helped. Father Rother's life was threatened, but he wrote, "At the first signs of danger, the shepherd can't run and leave the sheep to fend for themselves." On July 28, 1981, three men came and murdered him. His heart is now buried in the church there, among the people he loved.

◀ A PSALM FOR JULY

turn to
page 49

◀ READING

2 Corinthians 8:7, 9, 13–14

Listen to the words of the apostle Paul.

Brothers and sisters: You do everything better than anyone else. You have stronger faith. You speak better and know more. You are eager to give, and you love us better. Now you must give more generously than anyone else. You know that our Lord Jesus Christ was kind enough to give up all his riches and become poor, so that you could become rich. I am not trying to make life easier for others by making life harder for you. But it is only fair for you to share with them when you have so much, and they have so little. Later, when they have more than enough, and you are in need, they can share with you. Then everyone will have a fair share.

The word of the Lord.

■ REFLECTION

In what ways am I rich? How do I share what I have? The Catholics of Oklahoma send priests, teachers, and supplies to Guatemala. How do Catholics of my area support the missions?

■ CLOSING

Let us remember these intentions:

Loving God,
    we thank you for sending your disciples
    into the whole world,
    with your gifts of food and love.
Show us how to share what we have been given,
    and to be your worthy disciples.
We ask this through Christ our Lord. Amen.

Let us pray with the words that Jesus taught us:

Our Father . . .

sing
"alleluia"

Today is the birthday of Terry Fox, a Canadian athlete who lost his leg to cancer. In 1980 he began a Marathon of Hope to raise money for cancer research, running on his artificial leg. But after 3,328 miles, he was too ill to continue. He died in 1981, at the age of 22.

■ INTRODUCTION

Today we remember Saint Martha, a disciple of the Lord. Martha lived in Bethany with her sister Mary and her brother Lazarus. Jesus visited them often when he was near Jerusalem, and they were very dear to him.

In today's reading, Martha brings a problem to Jesus. In the days when Jesus and his friends lived, women could not study with a rabbi, or sit with men when they discussed important matters. But Jesus wanted both men and women to study his words and take them to heart.

■ A PSALM FOR JULY

turn to
page 49

■ READING

Luke 10:38–42

Listen to the words of the holy gospel according to Luke.

The Lord and his disciples were traveling along and came to a village. When they got there, a woman named Martha welcomed him into her home. She had a sister named Mary, who sat down in front of the Lord and was listening to what he said.

Martha was worried about all that had to be done. Finally, she went to Jesus and said, "Lord, doesn't it bother you that my sister has left me to do all the work by myself? Tell her to come and help me!"

The Lord answered, "Martha, Martha! You are worried about so many things, but only one thing is necessary. Mary has chosen what is bes and it will not be taken away from her."

The gospel of the Lord.

■ REFLECTION

Was Jesus being fair to Martha? Why was Mary choice better? Am I ever so busy with my activities that I am rude to the people around me?

■ CLOSING

Let us remember these intentions:

Loving God,
    you have words to speak to us
    because we are your children,
    and you love us.
Keep us close to you always
    so that we can listen to your words.
We ask this through Christ our Lord. **Amen.**

Let us pray with the words that Jesus taught us

Our Father . . .

 sing
"alleluia"

On this day in 1890, Vincent van Gogh (van GO) died. He tried to be a preacher but failed, and then chose painting as a way of showing God's presence in all things. Loo through a book of his paintings today.

■ INTRODUCTION

Today we remember Saint Peter Chrysologus *(cris-AHL-uh-gus),* a deacon who lived in the fifth century. "Chrysologus" means "golden word." Peter was given this title because of his preaching, which brought people from miles around to hear him. Copies of some of his homilies still survive. They are very short, and some people wonder if it was their length and not their wisdom that drew people Sunday after Sunday!

His bishop asked Peter to go with him to Ravenna *(ruh-VENN-uh),* Italy. It was time to elect a new bishop for that city. By the time they got there, the bishop had decided that Peter was the right man for the job. Peter was elected, even though he was not a priest.

■ A PSALM FOR JULY

turn to
page 49

■ READING
Romans 10:9–10, 14–15

Listen to the words of the apostle Paul.

You will be saved, if you honestly say, "Jesus is Lord," and if you believe with all your heart that God raised him from death. God will accept you and save you, if you truly believe this and tell it to others.

How can people have faith in the Lord and ask him to save them, if they have never heard about him? And how can they hear, unless someone tells them? And how can anyone tell them without being sent by the Lord? The Scriptures say it is a beautiful sight to see even the feet of someone coming to preach the good news.

The word of the Lord.

■ REFLECTION

"Jesus is Lord" is a simple prayer that I can use many times each day. Do I remember to pray often? Must people be grown up before they can tell others about Jesus? Do I bring the joy and love of God with me wherever I go (whether my feet are a beautiful sight or not!)?

■ CLOSING

Let us remember these intentions:

Gracious God,
    through the gift of your Spirit,
    and the teaching of your apostles,
    we can proclaim with all your church
    that "Jesus Christ is Lord."
Strengthen in us the gift of faith.
We ask this through Christ our Lord. **Amen.**

Let us pray with the words that Jesus taught us:

Our Father . . .

sing
"alleluia"

The best way to find the meaning of the homily is to discuss it with your family after Mass on Sunday.

■ INTRODUCTION

Today we remember Saint Ignatius of Loyola, who lived at the court of King Ferdinand and Queen Isabella of Spain. He enjoyed wealth and glory until he was wounded in battle. As he spent the next painful months recovering, the only books he could find were about Christ and the saints. Ignatius decided to live his life for God's glory rather than his own.

When he was well, Ignatius gave his money to the poor, hung his sword at Our Lady's shrine, and became a man of prayer. He and his friends formed a religious order called the Society of Jesus, or "Jesuits" for short. They dedicated themselves to reforming and serving the church as teachers and missionaries. Today thousands of Jesuits around the world are inspired by the energy and wisdom of Ignatius.

■ A PSALM FOR JULY

▶ turn to
page 49

■ READING

Ephesians 1:3–6

Listen to the words of the apostle Paul.

Brothers and sisters: Praise the God and Father of our Lord Jesus Christ for the spiritual blessings that Christ has brought us from heaven! Before the world was created, God had Christ choose us to live with him and to be his holy and innocent and loving people. God was kind and decided that Christ would choose us to be God's own adopted children. God was very kind

to us because of the Son he dearly loves, and s we should praise God.

The word of the Lord.

■ REFLECTION

What spiritual blessings has God given me? Ho can I raise the level of love in my family today Adopted children are specially chosen by the parents. How are Christians like children adopte by God?

■ CLOSING

Let us remember these intentions:

God of grace and wisdom,
  you continually raise up good people
  who show with their lives
  that they follow a holy and loving God.
Let our lives be as true as our faith.
We ask this through Christ our Lord. **Amen.**

Let us pray with the words that Jesus taught us

Our Father . . .

 sing
"alleluia"

On this day in 1790, the United States Patent Offic opened. Many people thought it was a waste of taxpa ers' money because everything useful had already bee invented! On this day in 1877, Thomas Edison received patent on the phonograph. The phonograph is the ance tor of the CD player! Invent something today.

AUGUST

THE MONTH OF AUGUST

The eighth month is a time of harvest in the northern hemisphere. We enjoy fresh tomatoes, zucchini, peaches and other tasty fruits and vegetables. The church turns our eyes to the heavenly harvest with the feasts of the Transfiguration of the Lord (August 6) and the Assumption of the Virgin Mary (August 15). The Assumption is a holy day of obligation in the United States, and many parishes celebrate with processions, festivals, picnics or the blessing of produce.

From the end of July until the beginning of September, the "dog star," Sirius, rises and sets with the sun. The name Sirius means "burning," and it is the brightest star in the sky. It is part of the constellation Canis Major, which means "large dog." These hot, sultry days of late July and early August are often called the "dog days" of summer.

Temperatures can rise above 100 degrees during August, so we have set aside a day to think about the sun (August 12). It is not surprising that August is the traditional month for vacations. People enjoy taking time from work and heading to the mountains or the beach to cool off. If you take a trip this month, tuck this book into your backpack! Vacation is an excellent time to pray with the whole family. There are special prayers for travel (page 8), rain (page 6) and family gatherings (page 9).

Saint Helen (August 18) is credited with finding the cross of Jesus, and many saints remind us this month that the cross plays a central role in our lives as Christians: Edith Stein (August 9), Franz Jagerstatter (also August 9) and Maximilian Kolbe (August 14) died at the hands of the Nazis in World War II. Many thousands died in the atomic bombings of Hiroshima (August 6) and Nagasaki (August 9), also in World War II. Other August people who were executed are Nat Turner (August 21) and Margaret Ward (August 30). Anne Hutchinson (August 26) was exiled. We also remember the sisters who nursed the wounded during the Civil War (August 17).

Our apostle of the month is Bartholomew (August 24). Other New Testament saints remembered in August are Mary the mother of Jesus (August 15, August 22), John the Baptist (August 29), Joseph of Arimathea (August 31) and Nicodemus (also August 31).

With the end of August we turn toward September, which brings school and homework, alarm clocks and lunchrooms. To help ease us into the fall we can look forward to a nice long Labor Day weekend, and a hearty "Amen!" to a blessed summer!

A PSALM FOR AUGUST

PSALM 95:1–2, 4–7

▶ all make
the sign
of the cross

LEADER   O come, let us sing to the Lord;
make a joyful noise to the rock of our salvation.

ALL   **Let us come into God's presence with thanksgiving;
let us make a joyful noise with songs of praise!**

LEADER   In God's hands are the depths of the earth
and also the heights of the mountains.
The sea belongs to God who made it,
and the dry land, because God formed it.

ALL   **Let us come into God's presence with thanksgiving;
let us make a joyful noise with songs of praise.**

LEADER   O come, let us worship and bow down,
let us kneel before the Lord, our Maker!
For the Lord is our God,
we are the people of God's pasture,
the sheep of God's hand.

ALL   **Let us come into God's presence with thanksgiving;
let us make a joyful noise with songs of praise.**

LEADER   O come, let us sing to the Lord;
make a joyful noise to the rock of our salvation.

ALL   **Let us come into God's presence with thanksgiving;
let us make a joyful noise with songs of praise!**

LEADER   Glory to the Father, and to the Son,
and to the Holy Spirit:
as it was in the beginning, is now,
and will be for ever. Amen. Alleluia.

ALL   **Let us come into God's presence with thanksgiving;
let us make a joyful noise with songs of praise!**

▶ turn back to
Daily Prayer
for today

■ INTRODUCTION

Today we remember Saint Alphonsus Ligouri *(al-FON-sus lih-GOO-ree)*, a fine preacher who spoke of God's love in ordinary language so that everyone could understand. In the eighteenth century, many Catholics were concerned about their sinfulness. They felt unworthy to receive communion. Alphonsus reminded them of God's forgiveness. He said that the eucharist helps us to become holy; it is not a reward for perfection.

■ A PSALM FOR AUGUST

▶ turn to
page 83

■ READING

Luke 7:36, 37–39, 39, 41, 46–47, 48, 50

Listen to the words of the holy gospel according to Luke.

A Pharisee invited Jesus to have dinner with him. When a sinful woman in that town found out that Jesus was there, she bought an expensive bottle of perfume. Then she came and stood behind Jesus. She cried and started washing his feet with her tears and drying them with her hair. The woman kissed his feet and poured the perfume on them.

The Pharisee said to himself, "If this man really were a prophet, he would know what kind of woman is touching him! He would know that she is a sinner."

Jesus turned toward the woman and said to the Pharisee, "Have you noticed this woman? When I came into your home, you didn't give me any water so I could wash my feet. But she has washed my feet with her tears and drie them with her hair. You didn't even pour oliv oil on my head, but she has poured expensiv perfume on my feet. So I tell you that all her sin are forgiven, and that is why she has shown grea love." Then Jesus said to the woman, "Your sin are forgiven. Because of your faith, you are now saved. May God give you peace!"

The gospel of the Lord.

■ REFLECTION

How do I show my love for Jesus? Do I trus God to love me no matter what?

■ CLOSING

Let us remember these intentions:

Loving God,
 forgive us for the wrong we do,
 and give us your peace.
We ask this through Christ our Lord. **Amen.**

Let us pray with the words that Jesus taught us

Our Father . . .

 sing
"alleluia"

On this date in 1779, Francis Scott Key was born. 1812, he wrote a poem and named it "The Star-Spangle Banner." Sing the national anthem with your fami today—you can hit the high notes!

INTRODUCTION

Today we remember Saint Basil the Blessed, a patron of Russia. Some men and women choose unusual ways to serve God. Basil the Blessed is one of these.

He wandered naked through the streets of Moscow like a prophet, praying and bearing witness to the teachings of the gospel in startling ways. Sometimes he took things from shops and gave them to the poor. Once he handed Tsar Ivan the Terrible a piece of raw meat, to shame him for "drinking men's blood." While Basil's ways made many people uncomfortable, they saw that his words were true, and they named the great cathedral in the center of Moscow after him.

A PSALM FOR AUGUST

turn to
page 83

READING

Luke 12:35–37, 40

Listen to the words of the holy gospel according to Luke.

Jesus said to his disciples: "Be ready and keep your lamps burning just like those servants who wait up for their master to return from a wedding feast. As soon as he comes and knocks, they open the door for him.

"Servants are fortunate if their master finds them awake and ready when he comes! I promise you that he will get ready and have his servants sit down so he can serve them.

"So always be ready! You don't know when the Son of Man will come."

The gospel of the Lord.

■ REFLECTION

How did Basil the Blessed's actions wake people up? Are there people calling attention to God's message today? Am I awake to injustice in my world? Do I speak up when I see it?

■ CLOSING

Let us remember these intentions:

We thank you, Lord God,
    for sending us amazing prophets
    who waken us from selfishness,
    open our eyes to the needs of others,
    and remind us of your coming.
Inspire and comfort them
    through Christ our Lord. **Amen.**

Let us pray with the words that Jesus taught us:

Our Father . . .

sing
"alleluia"

Today is also the feast of Blessed Joan of Aza, mother of Saint Dominic (August 8). She was a woman of rare common sense and strong prayer. Hug your mother today in honor of Blessed Joan.

AUGUST 3

■ INTRODUCTION

Today we remember Flannery O'Connor, who died in 1964. She was a gifted writer who lived with her mother on a small farm in Georgia. Because of a painful illness, Flannery was only able to spend two hours a day at the work she loved, writing novels and short stories. So she became very disciplined, doing each thing with her whole attention as long as her energy lasted.

Her illness drew Flannery deeper into the mystery of Christ's suffering and resurrection. The people in her stories sometimes suffer, and sometimes sin, but they are all touched by God's grace. Her faith is reflected in her stories.

■ A PSALM FOR AUGUST

turn to
page 83

■ READING

2 Corinthians 4:16–5:1

Listen to the words of the apostle Paul.

Brothers and sisters: We never give up. Our bodies are gradually dying, but we ourselves are being made stronger every day. These little troubles are getting us ready for an eternal glory that will make all our troubles seem like nothing.

Things that are seen don't last forever, but things that are not seen are eternal. That is why we keep our minds on the things that cannot be seen.

Our bodies are like tents that we live in here on earth. But when these tents are destroyed, we know that God will give each of us a place to live. These homes will not be buildings that someone has made, but they are in heaven ar will last forever.

The word of the Lord.

■ REFLECTION

Do I complain too much when I don't feel wel
Do I put too much importance on how I look
Do I treat disabled people with kindness?

■ CLOSING

Psalm 139:13-

Let us remember these intentions:

O Lord, you formed my inward parts,
you knit me together in my mother's womb.
I praise you, for I am fearfully
    and wonderfully made.
Wonderful are your works!
My frame was not hidden from you,
when I was being made in secret.
Wonderful are your works!

Let us pray with the words that Jesus taught u

Our Father . . .

sing
"alleluia"

On this day in 1492, Columbus and his little fleet of shi
set sail from Palos, Spain. This is a day to set off on
adventure. Perhaps you too will find more than yo
expect. What new world would you like to discover?

▌ INTRODUCTION

Today we remember John Vianney *(vee-ANN-e)*, who failed his seminary exams. But John's bishop saw that he was a holy man with a strong desire to serve God, so he ordained him anyway. John was sent to a tiny parish in Ars *(ahrz)*. Most of its 250 members had given up their faith during the French Revolution. John worked very hard to help them find it again. People soon began to realize that their pastor was a truly holy man.

John was especially good in the sacrament of reconciliation. He listened carefully to each person's story. He gave them advice and prayed with them. Word of the holy pastor (that word in French is *curé*) of Ars spread, and people came to him from all around. Soon the railroad had to run special trains to the little town. John Vianney, the patron of parish priests, died in the year 1859.

◀ A PSALM FOR AUGUST

 turn to
page 83

▌ READING   Ephesians 4:31–5:2

Listen to the words of the apostle Paul.

Brothers and sisters: Stop being bitter and angry and mad at others. Don't yell at one another or curse each other or ever be rude. Instead, be kind and merciful, and forgive others, just as God forgave you because of Christ.

Do as God does. After all, you are his dear children. Let love be your guide. Christ loved us and offered his life for us as a sacrifice that pleases God.

The word of the Lord.

■ REFLECTION

Do I let anger sometimes rule my actions and my words? Do I say things to people that I should not? Have I learned to forgive others with the same generous spirit that I want them to show me? Do I make use of the sacrament of reconciliation to come to know God better?

■ CLOSING

Let us remember these intentions:

Lord God, we thank you
    for sending priests to the whole world
    with gifts of forgiveness and healing.
We welcome those who bring your good news.
We pray for them and listen to their teaching.
Protect and guide them now and for ever.
We ask this through Christ our Lord. **Amen.**

Let us pray with the words that Jesus taught us:

Our Father . . .

 sing
"alleluia"

On this day in 1985, 40 years after atomic bombs were dropped on Japan, more than 100,000 people wrapped a bright fabric "Peace Ribbon" around the Pentagon. Pieces of the ribbon came from all over the world, and portrayed what would be lost in a nuclear war.

AUGUST 5

■ INTRODUCTION

On this day in 1909, Blessed Mary McKillop died after many years of illness. She was born in Melbourne, Australia, and began a religious order named the Sisters of Saint Joseph. They opened free schools and served the poor in other ways as well. Their unselfish work won the respect of people of all religions.

It was usual for bishops to decide the mission and rules for women religious, but Mother Mary received permission from the pope for her sisters to govern themselves. Because of this some bishops tried to interfere with her work and even spread stories against her. It caused Mother Mary great suffering, but instead of becoming bitter, she tried to accept it as willingly as Jesus had accepted his cross.

■ A PSALM FOR AUGUST

turn to page 83

■ READING

Hebrews 12:1–3

Listen to the words of the book of Hebrews.

Brothers and sisters, such a large crowd of witnesses is all around us! So we must get rid of everything that slows us down, especially the sin that just won't let go. And we must be determined to run the race that is ahead of us.

We must keep our eyes on Jesus, who leads us and makes our faith complete. He endured the shame of being nailed to a cross, because he knew that later on he would be glad he did. Now he is seated at the right side of God's throne!

So keep your mind on Jesus, who put up wit[h] many insults from sinners. Then you won't ge[t] discouraged and give up.

The word of the Lord. **Thanks be to God.**

■ REFLECTION

What is the race that Paul writes about? Wha[t] sins do I have that "just won't let go"? Does th[e] fact that Jesus was mocked for being good giv[e] me courage when I am mocked?

■ CLOSING

Let us remember these intentions:

Loving God,
   you call us your children
   and remain with us in difficulties.
Defend us against evil.
Make us brave and faithful,
   and strengthen us in times of trouble.
We ask this through Christ our Lord. **Amen.**

Let us pray with the words that Jesus taught us[.]

Our Father . . .

sing "alleluia"

John Eliot was born on this day in 1604. He came wit[h] other Puritans to the Massachusetts Bay Colony, wher[e] he translated the Bible into the Algonquin (al-GAHN-kwin) language. He is called Apostle to the Indians.

88

AUGUST 6

■ INTRODUCTION

Today is the feast of the Transfiguration of the Lord. It is also the anniversary of the dropping of the atomic bomb on Hiroshima *(her-OH-shih-ma)*, Japan, in 1945.

This day holds two visions of the world. On a mountain, the apostles saw in Jesus a dazzling revelation of divine glory. They fell to the ground in awe. The second vision is also too brilliant to look at. In it, the atomic cloud reveals only death and destruction, sorrow and fear.

■ A PSALM FOR AUGUST

turn to
page 83

■ READING

Matthew 17:1–8

Listen to the words of the holy gospel according to Matthew.

Jesus took Peter and the brothers James and John with him. They went up on a very high mountain where they could be alone. There in front of the disciples Jesus was completely changed. His face was shining like the sun, and his clothes became white as light.

All at once Moses and Elijah were there talking with Jesus. So Peter said to him, "Lord, it is good for us to be here! Let us make three shelters, one for you, one for Moses, and one for Elijah."

While Peter was still speaking, the shadow of a bright cloud passed over them. From the cloud a voice said, "This is my own dear Son, and I am pleased with him. Listen to what he says!" When the disciples heard the voice, they were so afraid that they fell flat on the ground. But Jesus came over and touched them. He said, "Get up and don't be afraid!" When they opened their eyes, they saw only Jesus.

The gospel of the Lord.

■ REFLECTION

What does the voice tell us about Jesus? Do I obey the command to listen? How can my family work for peace and an end to violence?

■ CLOSING

Let us remember these intentions:

Loving God, you speak to us
   in the quiet of our hearts.
Speak of hope for our world.
Speak of your gift of salvation.
Speak to us, for we are listening.
We ask this through Christ our Lord. **Amen.**

Let us pray with the words that Jesus taught us:

Our Father . . .

sing
"alleluia"

Those who survived, but suffer the ill effects of the atomic bomb are called "hibakusha" *(hee-BAH-koo-shuh)*. We are all hibakusha, even if our bodies show no scars.

AUGUST 7

■ INTRODUCTION

Today we remember Saint Victricius *(vik-TREE-she-us)*, who died in 407. He and his friend Martin of Tours were Roman soldiers. When they decided to become Christians, they put down their weapons and refused to remain in the army. They were beaten and treated as deserters.

Victricius became a wandering preacher in what is now France, and then was elected bishop. He was known as a peacemaker. Later, he wrote of his life, "I inspired the wise with love of peace, I taught it to the teachable, I explained it to the ignorant, I imposed it on the obstinate, insisting on it in season and out of season."

■ A PSALM FOR AUGUST

turn to
page 83

■ READING

Zechariah 9:9–10

Listen to the words of the prophet Zechariah *(zek-uh-RYE-uh)*.

The LORD says this: Everyone in Jerusalem, celebrate and shout! Your king has won the victory, and he is coming to you. He is humble and rides on a donkey. He comes on the colt of a donkey.

I, the LORD, will take away war chariots and horses from Israel and Jerusalem. Bows that were made for battle will be broken.

I will bring peace to nations, and your king will rule from sea to sea. His kingdom will reach from the Euphrates River across the earth.

The word of the Lord.

90

■ REFLECTION

Why is it hard to think of kings who do not u: war or the threat of war? Do I prefer leade who are fierce in the schoolyard or neighbo hood? Is peacefulness the same as weaknes: Why is peacemaking so difficult, when all peop want to be at peace?

■ CLOSING

Psalm 97:1–2, 4–5

Let us remember these intentions:

The Lord reigns; let the earth rejoice;
let the many coastlands be glad!
Clouds and thick darkness surround the Lord
the Lord's lightnings light up the world;
the earth sees and trembles.
The heavens proclaim God's justice
and all the peoples behold God's glory.
Rejoice in the Lord, O you faithful,
and give thanks to God's holy name!
Amen. Alleluia!

Let us pray with the words that Jesus taught u

Our Father . . .

sing
"alleluia"

Victricius shares this feast with Pope Sixtus II, a martyr 258. He is included in one of the most famous paintin in the world, the *Sistine Madonna*, painted by Raphael about 1513.

INTRODUCTION

Today we remember Saint Dominic Guzman, a Spanish priest who was blessed with the gift of persuasion. In the early thirteenth century, many Christians had the wrong idea that all the things of this world, including the human body, were really works of the devil, not the good creation of our loving God. Dominic studied the gospel and the teachings of the church, and began preaching the truth. When others joined his work he formed the Order of Preachers, also called Dominicans.

A friend wrote that Dominic's face "was friendly and joyful. You could easily see his inward peace." Dominicans share in their founder's spirit of joy and his love of learning.

A PSALM FOR AUGUST

turn to
page 83

READING

Matthew 9:36–38, 10:5, 7–8

Listen to the words of the holy gospel according to Matthew.

When Jesus saw the crowds, he felt sorry for them. They were confused and helpless, like sheep without a shepherd. He said to his disciples, "A large crop is in the fields, but there are only a few workers. Ask the Lord in charge of the harvest to send out workers to bring it in."

Jesus sent out the twelve apostles with these instructions: "As you go, announce that the kingdom of heaven will soon be here. Heal the sick, raise the dead to life, heal people who have leprosy, and force out demons. You received without paying, now give without being paid."

The gospel of the Lord.

REFLECTION

Why is it important for people to pray and study before preaching? Who are the workers in the Lord's field today? Is my faith a gift I received without paying?

CLOSING

Let us remember these intentions:

Lord God, we thank you
  for sending preachers to the whole world
  with your story of loving creation.
We welcome those who bring your good news.
Give us, too, fitting words
  to tell of your wonders.
We ask this through Christ our Lord. **Amen.**

Let us pray with the words that Jesus taught us:

Our Father . . .

sing
"alleluia"

On this date in 1945, President Harry Truman signed the United Nations Charter, and our country joined the organization where all nations of the world can discuss their problems peacefully.

AUGUST 9

■ INTRODUCTION

Today we remember Blessed Edith Stein, who was born into a Jewish family. She lost her faith in God for many years. Then she came upon a friend's copy of the life of Saint Teresa of Avila and stayed up all night to finish it. By morning, she was convinced of the truth of all that she had read. She was baptized, and after many years of prayer, she became a nun. Edith explained that she was joined to Christ both through her Christian faith and her Jewish blood.

When Nazi soldiers arrested the Jews, Edith was taken too, although she was a Catholic and a nun. She was killed at Auschwitz, Poland, on August 9, 1942. Survivors told of her courage during the days before her death. She prayed, and consoled the terrified women and children around her.

■ A PSALM FOR AUGUST

 turn to page 83

■ READING

Luke 9:23–24

Listen to the words of the holy gospel according to Luke.

Jesus said to all the people, "If any of you want to be my followers, you must forget about yourself. You must take up your cross each day and follow me. If you want to save your life, you will destroy it. But if you give up your life for me, you will save it."

The gospel of the Lord.

■ REFLECTION

What does it mean to take up my cross and fo[l]low Jesus? What are some examples of forge[t]ting about myself in order to follow Jesus? Wh[y] is it important for Christians to remember th[e] persecution of the Jews in the 1930s and 1940[s]?

■ CLOSING

Let us remember these intentions:

Loving God,
May the cross be our comfort in trouble,
    our shelter in the face of danger,
    our safeguard on life's journey,
    until you welcome all people
    into our heavenly home.
We ask this through Christ our Lord. **Amen.**

Let us pray with the words that Jesus taught u[s]

Our Father . . .

 sing "alleluia"

On this day in 1943, Franz Jagerstatter (YAH-gerz-dot-te[r]) an Austrian farmer, was killed by the Nazis for refusi[ng] to serve in the army. For him, duty could not substitu[te] for conscience. Hours before his death, he wrote to h[is] wife and three young daughters, "May the heart of Jesu[s] the heart of Mary and my own heart be one hea[rt] bound together for time and for eternity."

AUGUST 10

◤ INTRODUCTION

Today we remember Saint Lawrence, a deacon who served the church of Rome. He was in charge of giving alms to the poor of the city. In 258 Lawrence was arrested and given three days to gather up the church's wealth and turn it over to the emperor. On the third day he appeared before the court, bringing with him a crowd of people who were poor, blind, sick or homeless. "Here," he said, "is the church's real treasure." He was immediately thrown onto a red-hot grill. But as a sign that he was not afraid to die for his faith, Lawrence said, "You can turn me over now. I am done on this side."

◤ A PSALM FOR AUGUST

turn to
page 83

◤ READING

Matthew 5:1–2, 6:19–21, 25–26

Listen to the words of the holy gospel according to Matthew.

Jesus' disciples gathered around him, and he taught them:

"Don't store up treasures on earth! Moths and rust can destroy them, and thieves can break in and steal them. Instead, store up your treasures in heaven, where moths and rust cannot destroy them, and thieves cannot break in and steal them. Your heart will always be where your treasure is.

"Don't worry about having something to eat, drink, or wear. Isn't life more than food or clothing? Look at the birds in the sky! They don't plant or harvest. They don't even store grain in barns. Yet your Father in heaven takes care of them. Aren't you worth more than birds?"

The gospel of the Lord.

◼ REFLECTION

What things do I value? How can the love of things cause people to be greedy or jealous?

◼ CLOSING

Let us remember these intentions:

O God, you are good and generous,
  giving plants for food
  and flowers for our delight,
  giving sunshine and rain
  for the growth of all living things.
Hear our song of thanksgiving,
  and free our hearts from endless desires.
We ask this through Christ our Lord. **Amen.**

Let us pray with the words that Jesus taught us:

Our Father . . .

sing
"alleluia"

This is a day to take stock of your treasure, and share something with those in need.

■ INTRODUCTION

Today we remember Saint Clare, the daughter of a wealthy family of Assisi. When she was eighteen, Clare heard Saint Francis preach and decided to lead a life of poverty and prayer as he did. So she put aside her fine clothes and jewelry, cut her hair and wore a sackcloth dress tied with a rope. Soon her convent was filled with women who shared her ideals. Her sisters are now called "Poor Clares."

Francis and Clare became close friends. He helped her create a way of life that had not been tried before. She gave him wise counsel when he was depressed.

■ A PSALM FOR AUGUST

▶ turn to page 83

■ READING

Luke 12:15–21

Listen to the words of the holy gospel according to Luke.

Jesus said to the crowd, "Don't be greedy! Owning a lot of things won't make your life safe." So Jesus told them this story: "A rich man's farm produced a big crop, and he said to himself, 'What can I do? I don't have a place large enough to store everything.' Later, he said, 'Now I know what I'll do. I'll tear down my barns and build bigger ones, where I can store all my grain and other goods. Then I'll say to myself, "You have stored up enough good things to last for years to come. Live it up! Eat, drink, and enjoy yourself.'"

"But God said to him, 'You fool! Tonight yo will die. Then who will get what you ha stored up?'

"This is what happens to people who store everything for themselves, but are poor in t sight of God."

The gospel of the Lord.

■ REFLECTION

What could this story tell us about mone About toys or clothes? Why are possessions t source of so much trouble between peopl How do I handle my money and possessions?

■ CLOSING

Let us remember these intentions:

Merciful God,
We have been cared for and protected.
We have eaten and been filled.
Show us, your children,
   how to share what we have been given.
We ask this through Christ our Lord. **Amen.**

Let us pray with the words that Jesus taught u

Our Father . . .

 sing "alleluia"

Celebrate friendship! Thank God for friends you can tr
and share your heart with.

AUGUST 12

■ INTRODUCTION

Today we celebrate "Brother Sun." He warms our planet and fills it with things necessary for life and growth. But during August, the sun may be a bit *too* generous. Hot sunny days can be scorchers, when gardeners long for cool rain.

The sun is many things to us, but above all it is our giant lantern. Light has come to represent joy, knowledge, innocence, love and life itself. The sun is a powerful icon of God, whom we call "Light of Light," and "Light of the World." We look forward to the end of the world, when, according to the Bible, God will be all the light we need.

■ A PSALM FOR AUGUST

turn to
page 83

■ READING

1 John 2:7, 8–13, 14.

Listen to the words of the first letter of John.

My dear friends! You can see the darkness fading away and the true light already shining. If we claim to be in the light and hate someone, we are still in the dark. But if we love others, we are in the light, and we don't cause problems for them. If we hate others, we are living and walking in the dark. We don't know where we are going, because we can't see in the dark.

Children, I am writing you, because your sins have been forgiven in the name of Christ. Parents, I am writing you, because you have known the one who was there from the beginning. Young people, I am writing you, because you are strong. God's message is firm in your hearts, and you have defeated the evil one.

The word of the Lord.

■ REFLECTION

What does John mean by "the true light [is] already shining"? How is having my sins forgiven like coming into the light?

■ CLOSING

Let us remember these intentions:

The Lord is our light and our salvation;
 whom shall we fear?
The Lord is the stronghold of our lives;
 of whom shall we be afraid?
May we walk in the light of the Lord,
 now and for ever. **Amen.**

Let us pray with the words that Jesus taught us:

Our Father . . .

sing
"alleluia"

On August 11 and 12, the earth's orbit takes us through a cloud of rocks left by a comet. If we look in the sky before dawn, we can see falling stars called "Saint Lawrence's tears" because they appear close to his feast day (August 10). It is also called the Perseid meteor shower.

AUGUST 13

■ INTRODUCTION

Today we remember Saint Radegund *(RAH-duh-goond),* who was born in 518. She was a German princess, captured at the age of twelve by the Franks and later married to their king. She was a good queen, caring for the poor and founding hospitals. But the king was a bad husband, unfaithful and abusive. Radegund left him and became a deaconess. She founded a monastery for men and women, and lived a long life there. Her monastery became famous for its devout and well-educated nuns and monks. It attracted artists and poets, and became a center of culture as well as religion.

Radegund is the patron of prisoners because she was a captive, of shoemakers because she cleaned and polished the other nuns' shoes, and of potters because she washed the convent dishes.

■ A PSALM FOR AUGUST

turn to page 83

■ READING

Isaiah 56: 1, 6–7

Listen to the words of the prophet Isaiah.

The LORD said, "Be honest and fair! Soon I will come to save you, and my saving power will be seen everywhere on earth.

"Foreigners will follow me. They will love me and worship in my name. They will respect the Sabbath and keep our agreement. Then I will bring them to my holy mountain and let them celebrate in my house of worship. Their sacrifices and offerings will all be welcome on my altar.

And my house will be known as a house of worship for all nations."

The word of the Lord.

■ REFLECTION

Isaiah thought it would be good to have people of many nations praying together. Do people of different languages belong to my parish? Do we celebrate with a variety of customs and food and music? Are people of all races invited to share their wisdom and their hopes?

■ CLOSING

Let us remember these intentions:

God of all nations and creator of all peoples,
    heal all that divides your children.
Teach us to live together in peace.
Give us one heart and one vision.
Make us one body in Christ Jesus,
    filled with the joy of your Holy Spirit.
We ask this through Christ our Lord. **Amen.**

Let us pray with the words that Jesus taught us.

Our Father . . .

sing
"alleluia"

Radegund's friend, Fortunatus *(FOR-too-NAH-tus),* was chaplain at the monastery. He wrote many fine hymns, including one that begins with the Latin words *Pange Lingua (PAHN-jay LING-gwa).* "Sing, my tongue, the song of triumph" is its first line.

INTRODUCTION

Today we remember Saint Maximilian Kolbe (max-i-MILL-yun KOHL-be), a Polish priest who is honored by the church for the brave and generous way he died.

Father Kolbe opened centers in Poland and Japan where he published religious newspapers and pamphlets. Many young priests joined his work. In 1941, he was arrested with other Polish leaders who would not support Nazi rule. He was sent to the Auschwitz prison camp, and endured cruel treatment there. He comforted other prisoners, and often gave his meager food away. When ten men were chosen for execution, Father Kolbe asked to take the place of one who had a wife and children. On August 14, Father Kolbe was executed.

A PSALM FOR AUGUST

turn to
page 83

READING

Isaiah 65:18–20, 21–22

Listen to the words of the prophet Isaiah.

The LORD says this:
Celebrate and be glad forever!
    I am creating a Jerusalem
        full of happy people.
I will celebrate with Jerusalem
        and all of its people;
there will be no more crying
        or sorrow in that city.
No child will die in infancy; everyone will live
        to a ripe old age.

My people will live
        in the houses they build;
they will enjoy grapes
        from their own vineyards.
No one will take away
        their homes or vineyards.

The word of the Lord.

REFLECTION

Why would victims of persecution be comforted by Isaiah's vision of heaven? Why do Christians pray, "thy kingdom come, thy will be done on earth"? What can I do to help build God's kingdom?

CLOSING

Let us remember these intentions:

Jesus, our brother,
teach us to be fearless and faithful,
    and lead us to share in your kingdom,
        where we may be joyful together,
        for ever and ever. **Amen.**

Let us pray with the words that Jesus taught us:

Our Father . . .

sing
"alleluia"

On this day in 1863, Ernest Thayer was born. In 1888 he wrote "Casey at the Bat." If you like baseball you will love this poem. Read it out loud today.

AUGUST 15

■ INTRODUCTION

Today we celebrate the Assumption of Mary, body and soul, into heaven. According to ancient tradition, Mary lived in the town of Ephesus (EF-uh-sus) after the ascension of Jesus. When she was dying, John, who was by then Bishop of Ephesus, sent word to the other apostles, who hurried to her bedside. But Thomas did not arrive until after the funeral. On opening the tomb so he could pay his respects, they were amazed to find lilies in place of the body of their "mother" and friend.

Christians keep this day as a harvest festival. Mary has been harvested into God's kingdom, and the earth's season of plenty has begun. Arrange fruits, vegetables and flowers on your table, or around an image of Mary. Bless the garden (see page 7), or visit a pick-your-own farm.

■ A PSALM FOR AUGUST

 turn to
page 83

■ READING

Revelation 12:1, 5–6, 10

Listen to the words of the book of Revelation.

Something important appeared in the sky. It was a woman whose clothes were the sun. The moon was under her feet, and a crown made of twelve stars was on her head. The woman gave birth to a son, who would rule all nations with an iron rod. The boy was snatched away. He was taken to God and placed on his throne. The woman ran into the desert to a place that God had prepared for her.

Then I heard a voice from heaven shout, "Ou God has shown his saving power, and God kingdom has come!"

The word of the Lord.

■ REFLECTION

What images of Mary do we have in our hom What does the Assumption of Mary tell m about the importance of my body? What do it tell me about the meaning of heaven?

■ CLOSING

Let us remember these intentions:

Mary, our mother,
   you sheltered Jesus in your own body,
      raised him with a mother's care,
   and followed him in faith.
With you, we celebrate God's saving love.

Hail Mary, full of grace . . .

Let us pray with the words that Jesus taught us

Our Father . . .

 sing
"alleluia"

The Litany of Loreto lists beautiful titles that come fro the Bible or traditions about Mary. Rewrite it, keepin titles that seem beautiful to you, and adding others. Dra pictures for your poem. Hang them around the kitche or wherever you pray this week.

INTRODUCTION

Today we remember a saint named Stephen. This particular Stephen's people were Magyars, a fierce tribe who settled in what is now Hungary. Stephen was crowned king in the year 1000. He invited teachers from other lands to teach his people farming, sewing, reading and building. He cared for the poor, and ruled justly. He built churches and filled them with images of Jesus and the saints. Stephen tried to see that his people truly understood Christ, and followed him with honest faith.

Today's reading tells about the person King Stephen was named after, a deacon of the early church.

A PSALM FOR AUGUST

 turn to
page 83

READING

Acts 6:1–2, 3, 5, 6, 8

Listen to the words of the Acts of the Apostles.

A lot of people were now becoming followers of the Lord. But some of the ones who spoke Greek complained that the Greek-speaking widows were not given their share when the food supplies were handed out each day.

The twelve apostles called the whole group of followers together and said, "My friends, choose seven men who are respected and wise and filled with God's Spirit. We will put them in charge of these things." This suggestion pleased everyone, and they began by choosing Stephen [and then six others]. Then the apostles prayed and placed their hands on the men to show that they had been chosen to do this work.

God gave Stephen the power to work great miracles and wonders among the people.

The word of the Lord.

■ REFLECTION

How are disagreements settled in my family? How does my nation call forth wise leaders like King Stephen of Hungary? How are deacons chosen for the church today?

■ CLOSING

Let us remember these intentions:

Loving God,
    send your Holy Spirit upon our leaders,
    that they may govern your people
    with wisdom and justice,
    and so prepare for the coming
        of your kingdom.
We ask this through Christ our Lord. **Amen.**

Let us pray with the words that Jesus taught us:

Our Father . . .

 sing
"alleluia"

School will be starting one of these days! Time to enjoy the last days of vacation and think about getting ready for a new school year.

■ INTRODUCTION

On this day in 1863, federal guns fired on Fort Sumter, marking the midpoint of the Civil War. Today we remember more than 600 nuns who left their convents, sometimes on a few hours' notice, to serve as nurses during that war.

The military hospitals were in confusion, and the sisters ended up cooking, cleaning and laundering, as well as nursing and acting as surgeons' assistants. Some went to the battlefields at night, searching among the dead for anyone still alive. They slept little, sometimes on the floor. Some became ill and were sent home; others died in their military hospitals. The love and care of the nursing sisters brought comfort, hope and dignity to the wounded and dying soldiers of both armies.

■ A PSALM FOR AUGUST

turn to page 83

■ READING

Ephesians 3:16–17, 19–21

Listen to the words of the apostle Paul.

God is wonderful and glorious. I pray that his Spirit will make you become strong followers and that Christ will live in your hearts because of your faith. Stand firm and be deeply rooted in Christ's love. I want you to know all about Christ's love, although it is too wonderful to be measured. Then your lives will be filled with all that God is.

I pray that Christ Jesus and the church will forever bring praise to God. His power at work in us can do far more than we dare ask or imagine. Amen.

The word of the Lord.

■ REFLECTION

Would others consider me a strong follower Christ? The nursing sisters probably did mo than they thought they could. In what way h God enabled me to do more than I thoug I could?

■ CLOSING

Let us remember these intentions:

Loving God,
 bless the sick and the dying,
 and all those who care for them.
Strengthen all your people
 to be joyful and generous
 with those who need their help.
We ask this through Christ our Lord. **Amen.**

Let us pray with the words that Jesus taught u

Our Father . . .

sing "alleluia"

On this date in 1786, Davy Crockett was born Tennessee. He was a frontiersman, soldier and U.S. ser tor, and he died defending the Alamo. Like Davy, let travel with a light pack and a light spirit.

INTRODUCTION

oday we remember Saint Helen, mother of the mperor Constantine. Helen did great works of arity and built hospitals and churches. She ent many years in the Holy Land, finding and rotecting the places where Jesus lived. But she best known for finding the cross of Jesus.

Helen understood well the meaning of the oss. Her husband divorced her and took a more olitically useful wife when he became emperor. was 14 years before their son Constantine gave elen a place at court. Saint Helen died in 330.

A PSALM FOR AUGUST

turn to
page 83

READING

Mark 6:1–5

sten to the words of the holy gospel according Mark.

sus returned to his hometown with his disci- es. The next Sabbath he taught in the Jewish eeting place.

Many of the people who heard him were nazed and asked, "How can he do all this? here did he get such wisdom and the power work these miracles? Isn't he the carpenter, e son of Mary? Aren't James, Joseph, Judas, d Simon his brothers? Don't his sisters still live re in our town?"

The people were very unhappy because of hat he was doing. But Jesus said, "Prophets e honored by everyone, except the people of their hometown and their relatives and their own family."

The gospel of the Lord.

■ REFLECTION

How was Helen like a prophet who was not appreciated in her own home? How does it make me feel when people in my family don't think I am important? Do I know about the good work members of my family do? Do I tell them that I think they are wonderful?

■ CLOSING

Let us remember these intentions:

Loving God,
   teach us to hear your message
   in the words of those around us.
We ask this through Christ our Lord. **Amen.**

Let us pray with the words that Jesus taught us:

Our Father . . .

sing
"alleluia"

On this day in 1920, the 19th Amendment to the U.S. Constitution was ratified, giving the vote to women. Boys: Ask a girl for her opinion today and listen with respect. Girls: Share a thoughtful opinion today even if you are not asked.

AUGUST 19

■ INTRODUCTION

Today we remember Saint John Eudes *(yood)*, a priest who helped to renew people's faith during troubled times. In seventeenth-century France, lay people did not live by the teachings of the gospel. Priests led lives distant from the people, and some led shocking lives. Father Eudes traveled all over the country preaching parish missions, which were something like the parish renewal programs of today. He was able to awaken a new sense of commitment among priests and the people they served.

John often preached on the mercy of God, and spread devotion to the Sacred Heart of Jesus. John began a religious community to care for reformed prostitutes. Today they serve young women who have committed crimes.

■ A PSALM FOR AUGUST

turn to
page 83

■ READING

James 1:17–18, 21–22, 25

Listen to the words of the apostle James.

Every good and perfect gift comes down from the Father who created all the lights in the heavens. He is always the same and never makes dark shadows by changing. He wanted us to be his own special people, and so he sent the true message to give us new birth.

You must stop doing anything immoral or evil. Instead be humble and accept the message that is planted in you to save you.

Obey God's message! Don't fool yoursel[f] by just listening to it. You must never stop loo[k]ing at the perfect law that sets you free. God w[ill] bless you in everything you do, if you listen an[d] obey, and don't just hear and forget.

The word of the Lord.

■ REFLECTION

How is Jesus the "true message" God has se[nt] to us? How does a just law set people free? D[o] obey the law of God that I have been taught?

■ CLOSING

Let us remember these intentions:

God of justice and mercy,
 your law is a gift and not a burden.
It guides us to live in peace with you,
 with each other
 and within ourselves.
Help us to keep your law with all our hearts.
We ask this through Christ our Lord. **Amen.**

Let us pray with the words that Jesus taught u[s]

Our Father . . .

sing
"alleluia"

Find an image of the Sacred Heart of Jesus. Reflect [on]
the way Jesus opens his heart to all who are sinful or so[r]rowful. What other images of Jesus are in your home?

INTRODUCTION

Today we remember Saint Bernard. He was born in 1090 to a noble family, and he received the best education available. At the age of 22, he decided to become a monk, and 31 of his relatives and friends joined him. Later he opened a whole new monastery at Clairvaux (clare-VOH) in France.

Bernard lived during a time of social upheaval, and he was often asked to steady the people's faith. He was a stirring preacher, a convincing teacher and a skilled peacemaker. Bernard wrote that life was "overrun everywhere by anxieties, suspicions, cares. There is scarcely an hour free from the crowd . . . and the troubles and cares of their business. I have no power to stop their coming and cannot refuse to see them, and they do not leave me even time to pray."

A PSALM FOR AUGUST

 turn to
page 83

READING
Ephesians 5:15–20

Listen to the words of the apostle Paul.

Brothers and sisters: Act like people with good sense and not like fools. These are evil times, so make every minute count. Don't be stupid. Instead, find out what the Lord wants you to do. Don't destroy yourself by getting drunk, but let the Spirit fill your life.

When you meet together, sing psalms, hymns, and spiritual songs, as you praise the Lord with all your heart. Always use the name of the Lord Jesus Christ to thank God the Father for everything.

The word of the Lord.

■ REFLECTION

In what ways are things unsettled today? How do I find out what the Lord wants me to do? Do I praise God with all my heart at church? Does my family sing and pray together? Do I remember to thank God for everything?

■ CLOSING

Let us remember these intentions:

God of perfect harmony,
    place your music deep in our hearts,
    and teach us the song of creation.
God of deep peace and of the quiet night,
    wake us each day to the song of your love.
We ask this through Christ our Lord. **Amen.**

Let us pray with the words that Jesus taught us:

Our Father . . .

 sing
alleluia

Saint Bernard shares this day with the prophet Samuel. Samuel was called by God when he was still a child, but no one would believe him. The priest kept saying, "Go back to sleep!" Do you ever have that problem? Read his story in the First Book of Samuel, chapter 3.

■ INTRODUCTION

Today we remember the first pope of the twentieth century, Saint Pius X. He never forgot the needs of working people. He belonged to a trade union, and urged all Catholics to work for a just society. He told priests to provide religious education for adults as well as children. He was convinced that devotion meant nothing without an understanding of Christian teaching. But Saint Pius X is best known for moving the age of first communion from twelve to seven. He urged everyone to receive the eucharist frequently.

■ A PSALM FOR AUGUST

turn to
page 83

■ READING

John 6:30, 31–35

Listen to the words of the holy gospel according to John.

The people asked, "What miracle will you work, so that we can have faith in you? When our ancestors were in the desert, they were given manna to eat. It happened just as the Scriptures say, 'God gave them bread from heaven to eat.'"

Jesus said, "I tell you for certain that Moses wasn't the one who gave you bread from heaven. My Father is the one who gives you the true bread from heaven. And the bread that God gives is the one who came down from heaven to give life to the world."

The people said, "Lord, give us this bread and don't ever stop!" Jesus replied: "I am the bread that gives life! No one who comes to me will

ever be hungry. No one who has faith in me w ever be thirsty."

The gospel of the Lord.

■ REFLECTION

Saint Pius X said that three things are importa frequent celebration of the eucharist, continu study of the faith, and work for justice in t world. How does my family carry out tho three aspects of Christian life?

■ CLOSING

Let us remember these intentions:

Loving God,
through the bread and wine of the eucharist,
　may we share in the life,
　death and resurrection of your Son Jesus.
We ask this through Christ our Lord. **Amen.**

Let us pray with the words that Jesus taught u

Our Father . . .

 sing
"alleluia"

On this day in 1831, Nat Turner, a slave, led an uprisi against slavery in Virginia. He was captured and hang on November 11. 30 years later, slavery was outlawed the United States. Pray for all those around the wo today who still struggle for freedom.

◼ INTRODUCTION

In this octave, or eighth day after the feast of the Assumption, we celebrate the Queenship of the Virgin Mary. We use the image of royalty and a heavenly kingdom to think about the important part Mary has in God's plan of salvation, and the glorious reward that she has received. We, too, are called to share in Christ's mission, resurrection and glory.

Like a good queen, Mary watches over the church, praying for all who seek God's kingdom. This is a good day to sing Mary's prayer, the Magnificat. Many people know it by heart.

◼ A PSALM FOR AUGUST

 turn to page 83

◼ READING

Luke 1:39–47

Listen to the words of the holy gospel according to Luke.

Mary hurried to a town in the hill country of Judea. She went into Zechariah's home, where she greeted Elizabeth. When Elizabeth heard Mary's greeting, her baby moved within her. The Holy Spirit came upon Elizabeth. Then in a loud voice she said to Mary:

"God has blessed you more than any other woman! He has also blessed the child you will have. Why should the mother of my Lord come to me? As soon as I heard your greeting, my baby became happy and moved within me. The Lord has blessed you because you believed that he will keep his promise."

Mary said, "With all my heart I praise the Lord, and I am glad because of God my Savior."

The gospel of the Lord.

◼ REFLECTION

Who praises and encourages me the way Elizabeth praised Mary? How is Mary's reply to Elizabeth a model for the church's prayer?

◼ CLOSING

Let us remember these intentions:

Mary, our mother,
    you sheltered Jesus in your own body,
      raised him with a mother's care,
    and followed him in faith.
With you, we celebrate God's saving love.

Hail Mary, full of grace . . .

Let us pray with the words that Jesus taught us:

Our Father . . .

 sing "alleluia"

This is a good day to do something to honor the "queen" of your household.

■ INTRODUCTION

Today we remember Saint Rose, who lived in Lima, Peru. She was nicknamed "Rose" because of her beauty, which her parents hoped would help her find a rich husband. But she did not want to marry. She wanted to spend her life in prayer. So she moved into a small hut and tended the family garden. She earned money by selling her flowers and embroidery. She turned a room of her parents' home into a free clinic for anyone who needed her care.

When Rose died in the year 1617, such great crowds gathered that the streets were clogged. Rose of Lima was the first person born in the Americas to be named a saint of the church.

■ A PSALM FOR AUGUST

turn to page 83

■ READING

Galatians 5:1, 13–14

Listen to the words of the apostle Paul.

Brothers and sisters: Christ has set us free! This means we are really free. Now hold on to your freedom and don't ever become slaves of the Law again.

My friends, you were chosen to be free. So don't use your freedom as an excuse to do anything you want. Use it as an opportunity to serve each other with love. All that the Law says can be summed up in the command to love others as much as you love yourself.

The word of the Lord.

■ REFLECTION

In what ways am I free? Do I serve my family with love, perhaps by cooperating with the family chores? What do I do for other people that I don't have to do? Do I pay attention to what others freely do for me, and thank them?

■ CLOSING

Let us remember these intentions:

Loving God,
   free us from sadness and worry.
Free us from jealousy and greed.
Free us from distractions in prayer.
Free us to follow you with all our hearts.
We ask this through Christ our Lord. **Amen.**

Let us pray with the words that Jesus taught us

Our Father . . .

sing "alleluia"

Rose was born just 50 years after the conquistadors (kon-KEES-tuh-doors) had conquered Peru. She was raised in the Spanish culture but she was part Inca. She saw the suffering of Indians who were forced to work in the gold and silver mines. She vigorously protested against the enslavement, the poverty and the suffering of the native peoples.

AUGUST 24

▌ INTRODUCTION

Today is the feast of the apostle Bartholomew (bar-THAL-uh-mew), called Nathanael (nuh-THAN-yell) in John's gospel. He was from Cana, and he had a low opinion of people from Nazareth (NAZ-uh-reth). Yet he went along to hear Jesus.

Legend says that Bartholomew preached in Armenia and was martyred there. Armenian Christians hold him in special honor.

▌ A PSALM FOR AUGUST

turn to page 83

▌ READING

John 1:43–49

Listen to the words of the holy gospel according to John.

Jesus decided to go to Galilee. There he met Philip, who was from Bethsaida (beth-SAY-duh), the hometown of Andrew and Peter. Jesus said to Philip, "Come with me."

Philip then found Nathanael and said, "We have found the one that Moses and the Prophets wrote about. He is Jesus, the son of Joseph from Nazareth." Nathanael asked, "Can anything good come from Nazareth?" Philip answered, "Come and see."

When Jesus saw Nathanael coming toward him, he said, "Here is a true descendant of our ancestor Israel. And he isn't deceitful." "How do you know me?" Nathanael asked. Jesus answered, "Before Philip called you, I saw you under the fig tree." Nathanael said, "Rabbi, you are the Son of God and the King of Israel!"

The gospel of the Lord.

■ REFLECTION

Do my parents or grandparents have stories about their call to be disciples? What words would I use to express my faith in Jesus?

■ CLOSING

Let us remember these intentions:

Gracious God,
   we proclaim with all your church
   that Jesus is the Son of God
   and King of Israel!
Strengthen in us this gift of faith.
We ask this through Christ our Lord. **Amen.**

Let us pray with the words that Jesus taught us:

Our Father . . .

sing "alleluia"

On Saint Bartholomew's Day, 1572, a riot broke out in Paris. Roman Catholics broke a peace treaty and began to murder Protestants. By October nearly 20,000 were dead throughout France. Pray about this sad day, and about the scandal of "religious" wars.

AUGUST 25

■ INTRODUCTION

Today we remember Saint Louis IX, king of France. He had the first Gothic buildings put up, and he enjoyed dining with Thomas Aquinas and other scholars of the University of Paris. But he was best known for bringing equal justice to rich and poor. He stopped the nobles and churchmen from abusing common folk. He was a model king, and in later times, when reform was needed, the French would call for justice "as it was in Saint Louis' time."

Louis enjoyed a happy marriage, the respect of the nobles and the love of his people. He led two crusades, and died in 1270, far from home.

■ A PSALM FOR AUGUST

turn to
page 83

■ READING

1 Kings 3:5–6, 6–12

Listen to the words of the first book of Kings.

One night the LORD God appeared to Solomon in a dream and said, "Solomon, ask for anything you want, and I will give it to you."

Solomon answered, "LORD God, I'm your servant, and you've made me king in my father's place. But I'm very young and know so little about being a leader. And now I must rule your chosen people, even though there are too many of them to count. Please make me wise and teach me the difference between right and wrong. Then I will know how to rule your people. If you don't, there is no way I could rule this great nation of yours."

God said, "Solomon, I'm pleased that yo asked for this. You could have asked for you enemies to be destroyed. Instead, you asked fo wisdom to make right decisions. So I'll mak you wiser than anyone who has ever lived o ever will live."

The word of the Lord.

■ REFLECTION

If I could ask God for anything, as Solomon di what would I ask for? What wise people do talk to when I have questions?

■ CLOSING

Let us remember these intentions:

Loving God,
 you called Louis and Solomon
 to be wise and upright leaders.
Fill us with love like theirs
 and the ability to know right from wrong.
We ask this through Christ our Lord. **Amen.**

Let us pray with the words that Jesus taught u

Our Father . . .

sing
alleluia

On this date in 1916, the National Park Service w formed. Reflect today on the wisdom of protecting t natural beauty of the land, and preserving the wilderne which is home for God's wild creatures.

■ INTRODUCTION

Today we remember Anne Hutchinson, a Pilgrim who came with her husband to Boston in 1634 and raised a large family. Anne was a midwife and knew the use of healing herbs. She also knew the Bible, and invited women to her home for prayer and religious conversation. But the ministers objected to women discussing things that they "could not understand." Above all, they objected to Anne's belief that it was a blessing and not a curse to be a woman.

She was put in prison and then exiled from the community. Other Pilgrims wanted her husband to remain, but he said that Anne was "a dear saint and servant of God." The family moved to Rhode Island.

■ A PSALM FOR AUGUST

turn to
page 83

■ READING

Mark 3:20, 31–35

Listen to the words of the holy gospel according to Mark.

Jesus' mother and brothers came [to the place where Jesus was,] and stood outside. Then they sent someone with a message for him to come out to them. The crowd that was sitting around Jesus told him, "Your mother and your brothers and sisters are outside and want to see you." Jesus asked, "Who is my mother and who are my brothers?" Then he looked at the people sitting around him and said, "Here are my mother and my brothers. Anyone who obeys God is my brother or sister or mother."

The gospel of the Lord.

■ REFLECTION

If all who obey God are my brothers and sisters, how should I treat them? With whom do I share religious conversation and prayer?

■ CLOSING

Let us remember these intentions:

Just and loving God,
　give your disciples throughout the world
　courage to follow you
　with all their heart.
We ask this through Christ our Lord. **Amen.**

Let us pray with the words that Jesus taught us:

Our Father . . .

sing
"alleluia"

On this date in 1873, Lee DeForest was born. He invented a wireless voice transmitter, but no one believed such a thing was possible. So he was arrested for fraud when he tried to raise money to produce his invention: the radio. Do something new and surprising today.

■ INTRODUCTION

Today we remember Saint Monica *(MAH-nih-kuh),* a strong Christian woman of North Africa. When her son, Augustine *(uh-GUSS-tin),* joined another religion, Monica never stopped praying that God would help him see things more clearly. And she never stopped teaching him the truth of the Christian faith.

After many years, Monica's prayers were answered. Augustine became a Christian. After her death, Augustine wrote that those who knew her greatly praised and honored God, "because they recognized [God's] presence in her heart, for the fruit of her holy life bore witness to this." Saint Monica died in 387.

■ A PSALM FOR AUGUST

turn to
page 83

■ READING

Matthew 7:7–11

Listen to the words of the holy gospel according to Matthew.

Jesus said, "Ask, and you will receive. Search, and you will find. Knock, and the door will be opened for you. Everyone who asks will receive. Everyone who searches will find. And the door will be opened for everyone who knocks.

"Would any of you give your hungry child a stone if the child asked for some bread? Would you give your child a snake if the child asked for a fish? As bad as you are, you still know how to give good gifts to your children. But your heavenly Father is even more ready to give good things to people who ask."

The gospel of the Lord.

■ REFLECTION

Like Monica, do I often pray for someone? Do I pray even when it does not seem that God is listening? Am I able to be still and peaceful, remembering that God is with me? Do I cause my parents unnecessary worry?

■ CLOSING

Let us remember these intentions:

Lord our God,
  you are merciful
  and you do not fail us.
Help us to pray without ceasing
  and to wait patiently for your coming.
We ask this through Christ our Lord. **Amen.**

Let us pray with the words that Jesus taught us.

Our Father . . .

sing
"alleluia"

On this day in 1910, Mother Teresa of Calcutta was born. She gave out cards that said, "The fruit of silence is prayer. The fruit of prayer is faith. The fruit of faith is love. The fruit of love is service. The fruit of service is peace. We have to start with silence!

AUGUST 28

▪ INTRODUCTION

Today we remember Saint Augustine, the son of Monica whose feast was yesterday. As a young man Augustine studied many philosophies *(fil-HS-oh-feez)* and religions, but he was never happy with what he found. Finally, after many years, God's word came to him and he realized the truth of the gospel. It changed his life.

Augustine was baptized, and he returned to his home in Africa. There he became a great bishop, preacher and writer. Perhaps no other writings except the Bible have had so great an influence on Christianity. His most famous book tells the story of his life. It is called *Confessions,* and it is the story of God's love pursuing him. You will probably read it someday.

▪ A PSALM FOR AUGUST

 turn to
page 83

▪ READING

I John 4:7–10, 10–12

Listen to the words of the first letter of John.

My dear friends, we must love each other. Love comes from God, and when we love each other, it shows that we have been given new life. We are now God's children, and we know him. God is love, and anyone who doesn't love others has never known God. God showed his love for us when he sent his only Son into the world to give us life. God sent his Son to be the sacrifice by which our sins are forgiven. Dear friends, since God loved us this much, we must love each other.

No one has ever seen God. But if we love each other, God lives in us, and God's love is truly in our hearts.

The word of the Lord.

▪ REFLECTION

Can my friends tell by the way I act that God lives in me? How can we encourage one another to be loving and not unkind to others? What saintly people do I know?

▪ CLOSING

Let us remember these intentions:

God of grace and wisdom,
   you continually raise up good people
   who show with their lives
   that they follow a holy and loving God.
Let our lives be as true as our faith.
We ask this through Christ our Lord. **Amen.**

Let us pray with the words that Jesus taught us:

Our Father . . .

 sing
"alleluia"

On this day in 1963, Dr. Martin Luther King, Jr. gave his "I have a dream" speech before 200,000 people in Washington, D.C. He helped bring light to the darkness of inequality and racism. What is your dream for the country? Do something to make your neighborhood a better place today.

■ INTRODUCTION

Today we remember the death of John the Baptist. John told people to be sorry for their sins and to turn to God with all their hearts. He baptized them as a sign of God's forgiveness.

John bravely told King Herod and his family that they, too, were sinful. King Herod had John put in prison. Today's reading continues the story of John. This is a day to consider how governments sometimes ignore the rights of citizens and act with great injustice.

■ A PSALM FOR AUGUST

➤ turn to
page 83

■ READING

Mark 6: 21–25, 26–28

Listen to the words of the holy gospel according to Mark.

Herod gave a great birthday celebration for himself and invited his officials, his army officers, and the leaders of Galilee. The daughter of Herodias *(her-ROW-dee-us)* came in and danced for Herod and his guests. She pleased them so much that Herod said, "Ask for anything, and it's yours! I swear that I will give you as much as half of my kingdom, if you want it."

The girl left and asked her mother, "What do you think I should ask for?" Her mother answered, "The head of John the Baptist!"

The girl hurried back and told Herod. The king was very sorry for what he had said. But he did not want to break the promise he had made in front of his guests. At once he ordered a guard to cut off John's head there in prison. The guard put the head on a platter and took it t the girl.

The gospel of the Lord.

■ REFLECTION

Do I become angry at people who tell me I a wrong? Do I try to get back at people? Do sometimes say or do things just to show off?

■ CLOSING

Psalm 71:1, 3,

Let us remember these intentions:

In you, O Lord, do I take refuge;
let me never be put to shame!
Be to me a rock of refuge,
a strong fortress, to save me,
for you are my rock and my fortress.
O God, be not far from me;
O my God, make haste to help me!

Let us pray with the words that Jesus taught u:

Our Father . . .

 sing
"alleluia"

Edmund Hoyle, a lawyer in London, England, wrote book of rules for a card game called whist. His book w very popular, and soon his name became a saying. If y are playing a game "according to Hoyle," you are playi by the rules. He died August 29, 1769.

AUGUST 30

■ INTRODUCTION

Today we remember Saint Margaret Ward, one of the forty English martyrs executed in the sixteenth century. She was a London housekeeper who brought food and clean clothes to a priest who was in prison. Eventually they planned an escape. The priest got away, but Margaret was arrested and so badly tortured that she was crippled.

At her trial Margaret denied committing an offense against Queen Elizabeth. The Queen would have done the same thing in similar circumstances, she said. She was offered her freedom if she would attend the Protestant church, but she refused. Margaret was condemned and, with several others, was hanged on August 30, 1588. They sang hymns and encouraged one another all along the road to their execution.

■ A PSALM FOR AUGUST

turn to page 83

■ READING

Luke 13:22, 29–30

Listen to the words of the holy gospel according to Luke.

As Jesus was on his way to Jerusalem, he taught the people in the towns and villages. Someone asked him, "Lord, are only a few people going to be saved?"

Jesus answered, "People will come from all directions and sit down to feast in God's kingdom. There the ones who are now least impor-

tant will be the most important, and those who are now most important will be least important."

The gospel of the Lord.

■ REFLECTION

What does this reading tell us about the housekeeper and the queen? What could it mean that people will come into God's kingdom from all directions?

■ CLOSING

Let us remember these intentions:

Just and compassionate God,
  grant us courage in persecution,
  endurance in charity,
  and equal respect for all.
We ask this through Christ our Lord. **Amen.**

Let us pray with the words that Jesus taught us:

Our Father . . .

sing "alleluia"

Labor Day is the last gasp of summer! Create a summery summary! Tape-record people's best memories of the summer, put things in a scrapbook, look at pictures you have taken, write a song or poem, write a letter telling someone the things you have done.

■ INTRODUCTION

On this last day of August we remember Saints Joseph of Arimathea (*a-ruh-muh-THEE-uh*) and Nicodemus. They were wealthy, important men in Jerusalem.

After the death of Jesus, Joseph obtained his body from Pilate and bought fine linen to wrap it in. Nicodemus bought a quantity of expensive spices, and together they buried the body in a new tomb that belonged to Joseph.

Today's reading is a conversation between Jesus and Nicodemus about baptism.

■ A PSALM FOR AUGUST

▶ turn to
page 83

■ READING

John 3:3–8

Listen to the words of the holy gospel according to John.

Jesus said, "I tell you for certain that you must be born from above before you can see God's kingdom!" Nicodemus asked, "How can a grown man ever be born a second time?"

Jesus answered, "I tell you for certain that before you can get into God's kingdom, you must be born not only by water, but by the Spirit. Humans give life to their children. Yet only God's Spirit can change you into a child of God. Don't be surprised when I say that you must be born from above. Only God's Spirit gives new life. The Spirit is like the wind that blows wherever it wants to. You can hear the wind, but you don't know where it comes from or where it is going."

The gospel of the Lord.

■ REFLECTION

What does baptism mean to me? Why does my family preserve baptismal certificates, clothes, pictures, or other signs of our baptisms?

■ CLOSING

Let us remember these intentions:

Blessed are you, Lord God.
On the day of our baptism,
    you brought us new life
    through water and the Holy Spirit,
Help us to live each day as your children.
We ask this through Christ our Lord. **Amen.**

Let us pray with the words that Jesus taught us

Our Father . . .

 sing
alleluia

According to a legend, Joseph of Arimathea caught blood that flowed from Jesus' side on Calvary and took it in cup (called a "grail") to England. When it was stolen, King Arthur and his knights set out to find it—and had some fabulous adventures.

Read a story today about the quest for the Holy Grail.

SUMMER HELP

Preparing for Sunday

Catholics ordinarily do not arrive at church "cold" on Sunday morning. They first prepare themselves to receive the word of God, both in the readings from sacred scripture and in the gifts of the eucharistic bread and wine. Preparation enables the family—children as well as adults—to participate in the celebration with more devotion and understanding. Children who know what to listen for and know some of the questions that a reading raises are likely to be more attentive in church.

At least one reading from each of the summer Sundays has been included in this book. To find the readings for any summertime Sunday you will need to know its designation (for example: 12th Sunday of Ordinary Time, Year B). This information is given in most parish bulletins and Catholic calendars. Next, look on the chart on the next page and find that Sunday's designation. In that row you will find the scripture citations, then the page number in this book. (Every Sunday has three readings prescribed for it by the church, one from the Old Testament, one from the letters of the New Testament, and one from the gospels. This book is not big enough to include all three readings for every Sunday. It does include at least one, though.)

Find the page in this book; then as a family read the Bible passage and discuss the reflection questions. Let the children know that many of the readings have been shortened for this book. The translation used in this book (the Contemporary English Version) is the same as that used in the *Lectionary for Masses with Children,* but not in the lectionary used at regular parish Masses.

Sundays of Ordinary Time Likely to Fall during Summertime

An example of how to use this chart:

uppose next Sunday is the 14th Sunday in Ordinary Time, in
ear B (you found that in the parish bulletin), and you want to
repare with your family. Look for "Year B" in bold print.
here it is! Now go down the column until you see "14th
unday." It says "Mark 6:1–6" in the next column, and "page
01" in the last column. So turn to page 101. There is the read-
g from the gospel of Mark, with reflections and a prayer. You
ill hear the same gospel reading at church, and by preparing
ead of time, you and your family will be able to receive the
ord with even more love and joy.

unday	Scripture Readings	In This Book
ear A		
0th Sunday	Matthew 9:9–13	page 21
1th Sunday	Exodus 19:2–6	page 68
	Matthew 9:36—10:8	page 91
2th Sunday	Jeremiah 20:10–12, 13	page 27
	Matthew 10:26–31	page 18
3th Sunday	Matthew 10:37–42	page 61
th Sunday	Zechariah 9:9–10	page 90
	Matthew 11:25–30	page 70
th Sunday	Isaiah 55:10–11	page 23
	Romans 8:18–23	page 43
	Matthew 13:1–9	page 24
th Sunday	Wisdom 12:13, 16–19	page 22
th Sunday	1 Kings 3:5, 7–12	page 108
	Matthew 13:44–52	page 33
th Sunday	Romans 8:35, 37–39	page 66
th Sunday	1 Kings 19:9, 11–13	page 76
th Sunday	Isaiah 56:1, 6–7	page 96
st Sunday	Matthew 16:13–20	page 42
nd Sunday	Matthew 16:21–25	page 37

Sunday	Scripture Readings	In this book
Year B		
10th Sunday	2 Corinthians 4:13—5:1	page 86
	Mark 3:20–26, 31–35	page 109
11th Sunday	Mark 4:30–34	page 50
12th Sunday	Mark 4:35–41	page 45
13th Sunday	Wisdom 1:13–15, 2:23–24	page 31
	2 Corinthians 8:7, 9, 13–15	page 77
14th Sunday	Mark 6:1–6	page 101
15th Sunday	Ephesians 1:3–10	page 80
16th Sunday	Jeremiah 23:3–6	page 67
17th Sunday	Ephesians 4:1–6	page 32
	John 6:1–15	page 40
18th Sunday	John 6:24–39	page 104
19th Sunday	Ephesians 4:30—5:2	page 87
20th Sunday	Ephesians 5:15–20	page 103
21st Sunday	John 6:60–69	page 63
22nd Sunday	James 1:17–18, 21–22, 27	page 102

Year C		
10th Sunday	Luke 7:11–17	page 25
11th Sunday	Luke 7:36–50	page 84
12th Sunday	Luke 9:18–24	page 92
13th Sunday	Galatians 5:1, 13–18	page 106
14th Sunday	Luke 10:1–9	page 54
15th Sunday	Deuteronomy 30:10–14	page 73
	Luke 10:25–37	page 72
16th Sunday	Luke 10:38–42	page 78
17th Sunday	Luke 11:1–10	page 36
18th Sunday	Luke 12:16–21	page 94
19th Sunday	Luke 12:35–40	page 85
20th Sunday	Hebrews 12:1–4	page 88
21st Sunday	Luke 13:22–30	page 113
22nd Sunday	Luke 14:1, 7–14	page 62

Catholic Prayers

Our Father

Our Father,
who art in heaven,
hallowed be thy name;
thy kingdom come;
thy will be done on earth as it is in heaven.
Give us this day our daily bread;
and forgive us our trespasses
as we forgive those who trespass against us;
and lead us not into temptation,
but deliver us from evil.
Amen.

Hail Mary

Hail, Mary, full of grace!
The Lord is with you.
Blessed are you among women,
and blessed is the fruit of your womb, Jesus.

Holy Mary, Mother of God,
pray for us sinners,
now and at the hour of our death. Amen.

Glory to God

Glory to God in the highest,
   and peace to his people on earth.
Lord God, heavenly king,
almighty God, and Father,
   we worship you,
   we give you thanks,
   we praise you for your glory.
Lord Jesus Christ, only Son of the Father,
Lord God, Lamb of God,
you take away the sin of the world:
   have mercy on us!
You are seated at the right hand of the Father:
   receive our prayer!
For you alone are the Holy One,
you alone are the Lord,
you alone are the Most High,
Jesus Christ,
with the Holy Spirit
in the glory of God the Father. Amen.

Holy, Holy, Holy

Holy, holy, holy Lord,
God of power and might!
Heaven and earth are full of your glory.
Hosanna in the highest!
Blessed is he who comes
      in the name of the Lord!
Hosanna in the highest!

The Angelus

This prayer is often said at noon and at six o'clock in the evening, and sometimes church bells ring to remind us. It can be prayed in parts. The Hail Mary is on page 118. It's customary to bow when you come to the words, "And the Word became flesh."

LEADER:
The angel spoke God's message to Mary
ALL:
and she conceived of the Holy Spirit.
LEADER:
Hail, Mary . . .
ALL:
Holy Mary . . .

LEADER:
"I am the lowly servant of the Lord:
ALL:
let it be done to me according to your word."
LEADER:
Hail, Mary . . .
ALL:
Holy Mary . . .

LEADER:
And the Word became flesh
ALL:
and lived among us.
LEADER:
Hail, Mary . . .
ALL:
Holy Mary . . .

LEADER:
Pray for us, holy Mother of God,

ALL:
**that we may become worthy
of the promises of Christ.**

LEADER:
Let us pray.

Lord,
fill our hearts with your grace:
once, through the message of an angel
you revealed to us the incarnation of your Son;
now, through his suffering and death
lead us to the glory of his resurrection.
We ask this through Christ our Lord.
ALL:
Amen.

Eternal Rest

This prayer is good when we remember those who have died.

LEADER:
Eternal rest grant unto them, O Lord,
ALL:
and let perpetual light shine upon them.

LEADER:
May they rest in peace.
ALL:
Amen.

LEADER:
May their souls,
and the souls of all the faithful departed,
through the mercy of God,
rest in peace.
ALL:
Amen.

The People in This Book